A TRAVEL JOURNAL

LAUGHING ELEPHANT   2000

IDENTIFICATION

NAME:

ADDRESS:

TELEPHONE:

E-MAIL:

PASSPORT #:

EMERGENCY CONTACT:

COMPANIONS

NAME:

NAME:

NAME:

NAME:

NAME:

Los Angeles Biltmore

ITINERARY

DAY 1:	
DAY 2:	
DAY 3:	
DAY 4:	
DAY 5:	
DAY 6:	
DAY 7:	
DAY 8:	
DAY 9:	
DAY 10:	
DAY 11:	
DAY 12:	
DAY 13:	
DAY 14:	
DAY 15:	
DAY 16:	
DAY 17:	
DAY 18:	
DAY 19:	
DAY 20:	
DAY 21:	
DAY 22:	
DAY 23:	
DAY 24:	
DAY 25:	
DAY 26:	
DAY 27:	
DAY 28:	

WEEK

TRAIN TICKETSPHOTOGRAPHSRECIEPTSBEVERAG
ECOASTERSMATCHBOOKSLEAVESBROCHURESPA
PER CURRENCYSUBWAY TICKETSMUSEUM PASSES
BUSINESS CARDSTOLLBOOTH RECIEPTSPRESSED F
LOWERSCANDY WRAPPERSMAPSWINE LABELSLU
GGAGE TAGSHOTEL STATIONARYFERRY TICKETSP
HONECARDSMOVIE & THEATER TICKETSMENUSPA
SSPORT PHOTOSPARKING TICKETSTRAIN TICKETS
PHOTOGRAPHSRECIEPTSBEVERAGECOASTERSM
ATCHBOOKSLEAVESBROCHURESPAPER CURRENC
YSUBWAY TICKETSMUSEUM PASSESBUSINESS CA
RDSTOLLBOOTH RECIEPTSPRESSED FLOWERSCAN
DY WRAPPERSMAPSWINE LABELSLUGGAGE TAGS
HOTEL STATIONARYFERRY TICKETSPHONECARDS
MOVIE & THEATER TICKETSMENUSPASSPORT PHC
TOSPARKING TICKETSTRAIN TICKETSPHOTOGRAP
HSRECIEPTSBEVERAGECOASTERSMATCHBOOKSL
EAVESBROCHURESPAPER CURRENCYSUBWAY TIC
KETSMUSEUM PASSESBUSINESS CARDSTOLLBOC
TH RECIEPTSPRESSED FLOWERSCANDY WRAPPER
SMAPSWINE LABELSLUGGAGE TAGSHOTEL STAT
ONARYFERRY TICKETSPHONECARDSMOVIE & THE
ATER TICKETSMENUSPASSPORT PHOTOSPARKING
TICKETSTRAIN TICKETSPHOTOGRAPHSRECIEPTSB
EVERAGECOASTERSMATCHBOOKSLEAVESBROC
HURESPAPER CURRENCYSUBWAY TICKETSMUSEU
M PASSESBUSINESS CARDSTOLLBOOTH RECIEPTS
PRESSED FLOWERSCANDY WRAPPERSMAPSWINE
LABELSLUGGAGE TAGSHOTEL STATIONARYFERRY
TICKETSPHONECARDSMOVIE & THEATER TICKETS
MENUSPASSPORT PHOTOSPARKING TICKETSTRA
N TICKETSPHOTOGRAPHSRECIEPTSBEVERAGECC
ASTERSMATCHBOOKSLEAVESBROCHURESPAPER
CURRENCYSUBWAY TICKETSMUSEUM PASSESBUS
INESS CARDSTOLLBOOTH RECIEPTSPRESSED FLC
WERSCANDY WRAPPERSMAPSWINE LABELSLUG
GAGE TAGSHOTEL STATIONARYFERRY TICKETSPH
ONECARDSMOVIE & THEATER TICKETSMENUSPA
SPORT PHOTOSPARKING TICKETSTRAIN TICKETSP

PASTE HERE

DATE: _____

_____

LOCATION: _____

_____

LODGING: _____

_____

TRANSPORTATION: _____

_____

_____

PLACES VISITED: _____

_____

_____

_____

_____

_____

_____

MEALS, RESTAURANTS, SPECIAL DISHES: _____

_____

_____

_____

_____

_____

_____

_____

TRAIN TICKETSPHOTOGRAPHSRECIEPTSBEVERAG
ECOASTERSMATCHBOOKSLEAVESBROCHURESPA
PER CURRENCYSUBWAY TICKETSMUSEUM PASSES
BUSINESS CARDSTOLLBOOTH RECIEPTSPRESSED F
LOWERSCANDY WRAPPERSMAPSWINE LABELSLU
GGAGE TAGSHOTEL STATIONARYFERRY TICKETSP
HONECARDSMOVIE & THEATER TICKETSMENUSPA
SSPORT PHOTOSPARKING TICKETSTRAIN TICKETS
PHOTOGRAPHSRECIEPTSBEVERAGECOASTERSM
ATCHBOOKSLEAVESBROCHURESPAPER CURRENC
YSUBWAY TICKETSMUSEUM PASSESBUSINESS CA
RDSTOLLBOOTH RECIEPTSPRESSED FLOWERSCAN
DY WRAPPERSMAPSWINE LABELSLUGGAGE TAGS
HOTEL STATIONARYFERRY TICKETSPHONECARDS
MOVIE & THEATER TICKETSMENUSPASSPORT PHO
TOSPARKING TICKETSTRAIN TICKETSPHOTOGRAP
HSRECIEPTSBEVERAGECOASTERSMATCHBOOKSL
EAVESBROCHURESPAPER CURRENCYSUBWAY TIC
KETSMUSEUM PASSESBUSINESS CARDSTOLLBOO
TH RECIEPTSPRESSED FLOWERSCANDY WRAPPER
SMAPSWINE LABELSLUGGAGE TAGSHOTEL STATI
ONARYFERRY TICKETSPHONECARDSMOVIE & THE
ATER TICKETSMENUSPASSPORT PHOTOSPARKING
TICKETSTRAIN TICKETSPHOTOGRAPHSRECIEPTSB
EVERAGECOASTERSMATCHBOOKSLEAVESBROC
HURESPAPER CURRENCYSUBWAY TICKETSMUSEU
M PASSESBUSINESS CARDSTOLLBOOTH RECIEPTS
PRESSED FLOWERSCANDY WRAPPERSMAPSWINE
LABELSLUGGAGE TAGSHOTEL STATIONARYFERRY
TICKETSPHONECARDSMOVIE & THEATER TICKETS
MENUSPASSPORT PHOTOSPARKING TICKETSTRAI
N TICKETSPHOTOGRAPHSRECIEPTSBEVERAGECO
ASTERSMATCHBOOKSLEAVESBROCHURESPAPER
CURRENCYSUBWAY TICKETSMUSEUM PASSESBUS
INESS CARDSTOLLBOOTH RECIEPTSPRESSED FLO
WERSCANDY WRAPPERSMAPSWINE LABELSLUG
GAGE TAGSHOTEL STATIONARYFERRY TICKETSPH
ONECARDSMOVIE & THEATER TICKETSMENUSPAS
SPORT PHOTOSPARKING TICKETSTRAIN TICKETSP

PASTE HERE

INTERESTING SHOPS:

_____

_____

_____

_____

ACQUISITIONS & GIFTS:

_____

_____

_____

_____

THINGS TOO LARGE, FRAGILE OR EXPENSIVE TO BUY:

_____

_____

_____

_____

NOTEWORTHY SIGHTS OR EXPERIENCES:

_____

_____

_____

_____

MEMORABLE ENCOUNTERS:

_____

_____

_____

_____

_____

TRAIN TICKETSPHOTOGRAPHSRECIEPTSBEVERAG
ECOASTERSMATCHBOOKSLEAVESBROCHURESPA
PER CURRENCYSUBWAY TICKETSMUSEUM PASSES
BUSINESS CARDSTOLLBOOTH RECIEPTSPRESSED F
LOWERSCANDY WRAPPERSMAPSWINE LABELSLU
GGAGE TAGSHOTEL STATIONARYFERRY TICKETSP
HONECARDSMOVIE & THEATER TICKETSMENUSPA
SSPORT PHOTOSPARKING TICKETSTRAIN TICKETS
PHOTOGRAPHSRECIEPTSBEVERAGECOASTERSM
ATCHBOOKSLEAVESBROCHURESPAPER CURRENC
YSUBWAY TICKETSMUSEUM PASSESBUSINESS CA
RDSTOLLBOOTH RECIEPTSPRESSED FLOWERSCAN
DY WRAPPERSMAPSWINE LABELSLUGGAGE TAGS
HOTEL STATIONARYFERRY TICKETSPHONECARDS
MOVIE & THEATER TICKETSMENUSPASSPORT PHO
TOSPARKING TICKETSTRAIN TICKETSPHOTOGRAP
HSRECIEPTSBEVERAGECOASTERSMATCHBOOKSL
EAVESBROCHURESPAPER CURRENCYSUBWAY TIC
KETSMUSEUM PASSESBUSINESS CARDSTOLLBOO
TH RECIEPTSPRESSED FLOWERSCANDY WRAPPER
SMAPSWINE LABELSLUGGAGE TAGSHOTEL STATI
ONARYFERRY TICKETSPHONECARDSMOVIE & THE
ATER TICKETSMENUSPASSPORT PHOTOSPARKING
TICKETSTRAIN TICKETSPHOTOGRAPHSRECIEPTSB
EVERAGECOASTERSMATCHBOOKSLEAVESBROC
HURESPAPER CURRENCYSUBWAY TICKETSMUSEU
M PASSESBUSINESS CARDSTOLLBOOTH RECIEPTS
PRESSED FLOWERSCANDY WRAPPERSMAPSWINE
LABELSLUGGAGE TAGSHOTEL STATIONARYFERRY
TICKETSPHONECARDSMOVIE & THEATER TICKETS
MENUSPASSPORT PHOTOSPARKING TICKETSTRAI
N TICKETSPHOTOGRAPHSRECIEPTSBEVERAGECO
ASTERSMATCHBOOKSLEAVESBROCHURESPAPER
CURRENCYSUBWAY TICKETSMUSEUM PASSESBUS
INESS CARDSTOLLBOOTH RECIEPTSPRESSED FLO
WERSCANDY WRAPPERSMAPSWINE LABELSLUG
GAGE TAGSHOTEL STATIONARYFERRY TICKETSPH
ONECARDSMOVIE & THEATER TICKETSMENUSPAS
SPORT PHOTOSPARKING TICKETSTRAIN TICKETSP

PASTE HERE

DATE:

DAY 2 AY

HOTELS MARHABA

LOCATION:

LODGING:

TRANSPORTATION:

PLACES VISITED:

MEALS, RESTAURANTS, SPECIAL DISHES:

TRAIN TICKETSPHOTOGRAPHSRECIEPTSBEVERAG
ECOASTERSMATCHBOOKSLEAVESBROCHURESPA
PER CURRENCYSUBWAY TICKETSMUSEUM PASSES
BUSINESS CARDSTOLLBOOTH RECIEPTSPRESSED F
LOWERSCANDY WRAPPERSMAPSWINE LABELSLU
GGAGE TAGSHOTEL STATIONARYFERRY TICKETSP
HONECARDSMOVIE & THEATER TICKETSMENUSPA
SSPORT PHOTOSPARKING TICKETSTRAIN TICKETS
PHOTOGRAPHSRECIEPTSBEVERAGECOASTERSM
ATCHBOOKSLEAVESBROCHURESPAPER CURRENC
YSUBWAY TICKETSMUSEUM PASSESBUSINESS CA
RDSTOLLBOOTH RECIEPTSPRESSED FLOWERSCAN
DY WRAPPERSMAPSWINE LABELSLUGGAGE TAGS
HOTEL STATIONARYFERRY TICKETSPHONECARDS
MOVIE & THEATER TICKETSMENUSPASSPORT PHO
TOSPARKING TICKETSTRAIN TICKETSPHOTOGRAP
HSRECIEPTSBEVERAGECOASTERSMATCHBOOKSL
EAVESBROCHURESPAPER CURRENCYSUBWAY TIC
KETSMUSEUM PASSESBUSINESS CARDSTOLLBOO
TH RECIEPTSPRESSED FLOWERSCANDY WRAPPER
SMAPSWINE LABELSLUGGAGE TAGSHOTEL STATI
ONARYFERRY TICKETSPHONECARDSMOVIE & THE
ATER TICKETSMENUSPASSPORT PHOTOSPARKING
TICKETSTRAIN TICKETSPHOTOGRAPHSRECIEPTSB
EVERAGECOASTERSMATCHBOOKSLEAVESBROC
HURESPAPER CURRENCYSUBWAY TICKETSMUSEU
M PASSESBUSINESS CARDSTOLLBOOTH RECIEPTS
PRESSED FLOWERSCANDY WRAPPERSMAPSWINE
LABELSLUGGAGE TAGSHOTEL STATIONARYFERRY
TICKETSPHONECARDSMOVIE & THEATER TICKETS
MENUSPASSPORT PHOTOSPARKING TICKETSTRAI
N TICKETSPHOTOGRAPHSRECIEPTSBEVERAGECO
ASTERSMATCHBOOKSLEAVESBROCHURESPAPER
CURRENCYSUBWAY TICKETSMUSEUM PASSESBUS
INESS CARDSTOLLBOOTH RECIEPTSPRESSED FLO
WERSCANDY WRAPPERSMAPSWINE LABELSLUG
GAGE TAGSHOTEL STATIONARYFERRY TICKETSPH
ONECARDSMOVIE & THEATER TICKETSMENUSPAS
SPORT PHOTOSPARKING TICKETSTRAIN TICKETSP

PASTE HERE

INTERESTING SHOPS:

ACQUISITIONS & GIFTS:

THINGS TOO LARGE, FRAGILE OR EXPENSIVE TO BUY:

NOTEWORTHY SIGHTS OR EXPERIENCES:

MEMORABLE ENCOUNTERS:

TRAIN TICKETSPHOTOGRAPHSRECIEPTSBEVERAG
ECOASTERSMATCHBOOKSLEAVESBROCHURESPA
PER CURRENCYSUBWAY TICKETSMUSEUM PASSES
BUSINESS CARDSTOLLBOOTH RECIEPTSPRESSED F
LOWERSCANDY WRAPPERSMAPSWINE LABELSLU
GGAGE TAGSHOTEL STATIONARYFERRY TICKETSP
HONECARDSMOVIE & THEATER TICKETSMENUSPA
SSPORT PHOTOSPARKING TICKETSTRAIN TICKETS
PHOTOGRAPHSRECIEPTSBEVERAGECOASTERSM
ATCHBOOKSLEAVESBROCHURESPAPER CURRENC
YSUBWAY TICKETSMUSEUM PASSESBUSINESS CA
RDSTOLLBOOTH RECIEPTSPRESSED FLOWERSCAN
DY WRAPPERSMAPSWINE LABELSLUGGAGE TAGS
HOTEL STATIONARYFERRY TICKETSPHONECARDS
MOVIE & THEATER TICKETSMENUSPASSPORT PHO
TOSPARKING TICKETSTRAIN TICKETSPHOTOGRAP
HSRECIEPTSBEVERAGECOASTERSMATCHBOOKSL
EAVESBROCHURESPAPER CURRENCYSUBWAY TIC
KETSMUSEUM PASSESBUSINESS CARDSTOLLBOO
TH RECIEPTSPRESSED FLOWERSCANDY WRAPPER
SMAPSWINE LABELSLUGGAGE TAGSHOTEL STATI
ONARYFERRY TICKETSPHONECARDSMOVIE & THE
ATER TICKETSMENUSPASSPORT PHOTOSPARKING
TICKETSTRAIN TICKETSPHOTOGRAPHSRECIEPTSB
EVERAGECOASTERSMATCHBOOKSLEAVESBROC
HURESPAPER CURRENCYSUBWAY TICKETSMUSEU
M PASSESBUSINESS CARDSTOLLBOOTH RECIEPTS
PRESSED FLOWERSCANDY WRAPPERSMAPSWINE
LABELSLUGGAGE TAGSHOTEL STATIONARYFERRY
TICKETSPHONECARDSMOVIE & THEATER TICKETS
MENUSPASSPORT PHOTOSPARKING TICKETSTRAI
N TICKETSPHOTOGRAPHSRECIEPTSBEVERAGECO
ASTERSMATCHBOOKSLEAVESBROCHURESPAPER
CURRENCYSUBWAY TICKETSMUSEUM PASSESBUS
INESS CARDSTOLLBOOTH RECIEPTSPRESSED FLO
WERSCANDY WRAPPERSMAPSWINE LABELSLUG
GAGE TAGSHOTEL STATIONARYFERRY TICKETSPH
ONECARDSMOVIE & THEATER TICKETSMENUSPAS
SPORT PHOTOSPARKING TICKETSTRAIN TICKETSP

PASTE HERE

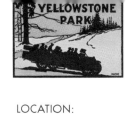

DATE:

LOCATION:

LODGING:

TRANSPORTATION:

PLACES VISITED:

MEALS, RESTAURANTS, SPECIAL DISHES:

TRAIN TICKETSPHOTOGRAPHSRECIEPTSBEVERAG
ECOASTERSMATCHBOOKSLEAVESBROCHURESPA
PER CURRENCYSUBWAY TICKETSMUSEUM PASSES
BUSINESS CARDSTOLLBOOTH RECIEPTSPRESSED F
LOWERSCANDY WRAPPERSMAPSWINE LABELSLU
GGAGE TAGSHOTEL STATIONARYFERRY TICKETSP
HONECARDSMOVIE & THEATER TICKETSMENUSPA
SSPORT PHOTOSPARKING TICKETSTRAIN TICKETS
PHOTOGRAPHSRECIEPTSBEVERAGECOASTERSM
ATCHBOOKSLEAVESBROCHURESPAPER CURRENC
YSUBWAY TICKETSMUSEUM PASSESBUSINESS CA
RDSTOLLBOOTH RECIEPTSPRESSED FLOWERSCAN
DY WRAPPERSMAPSWINE LABELSLUGGAGE TAGS
HOTEL STATIONARYFERRY TICKETSPHONECARDS
MOVIE & THEATER TICKETSMENUSPASSPORT PHO
TOSPARKING TICKETSTRAIN TICKETSPHOTOGRAP
HSRECIEPTSBEVERAGECOASTERSMATCHBOOKSL
EAVESBROCHURESPAPER CURRENCYSUBWAY TIC
KETSMUSEUM PASSESBUSINESS CARDSTOLLBOO
TH RECIEPTSPRESSED FLOWERSCANDY WRAPPER
SMAPSWINE LABELSLUGGAGE TAGSHOTEL STATI
ONARYFERRY TICKETSPHONECARDSMOVIE & THE
ATER TICKETSMENUSPASSPORT PHOTOSPARKING
TICKETSTRAIN TICKETSPHOTOGRAPHSRECIEPTSB
EVERAGECOASTERSMATCHBOOKSLEAVESBROC
HURESPAPER CURRENCYSUBWAY TICKETSMUSEU
M PASSESBUSINESS CARDSTOLLBOOTH RECIEPTS
PRESSED FLOWERSCANDY WRAPPERSMAPSWINE
LABELSLUGGAGE TAGSHOTEL STATIONARYFERRY
TICKETSPHONECARDSMOVIE & THEATER TICKETS
MENUSPASSPORT PHOTOSPARKING TICKETSTRAI
N TICKETSPHOTOGRAPHSRECIEPTSBEVERAGECO
ASTERSMATCHBOOKSLEAVESBROCHURESPAPER
CURRENCYSUBWAY TICKETSMUSEUM PASSESBUS
INESS CARDSTOLLBOOTH RECIEPTSPRESSED FLO
WERSCANDY WRAPPERSMAPSWINE LABELSLUG
GAGE TAGSHOTEL STATIONARYFERRY TICKETSPH
ONECARDSMOVIE & THEATER TICKETSMENUSPAS
SPORT PHOTOSPARKING TICKETSTRAIN TICKETSP

PASTE HERE

INTERESTING SHOPS:

ACQUISITIONS & GIFTS:

THINGS TOO LARGE, FRAGILE OR EXPENSIVE TO BUY:

NOTEWORTHY SIGHTS OR EXPERIENCES:

MEMORABLE ENCOUNTERS:

TRAIN TICKETSPHOTOGRAPHSRECIEPTSBEVERAG
ECOASTERSMATCHBOOKSLEAVESBROCHURESPA
PER CURRENCYSUBWAY TICKETSMUSEUM PASSES
BUSINESS CARDSTOLLBOOTH RECIEPTSPRESSED F
LOWERSCANDY WRAPPERSMAPSWINE LABELSLU
GGAGE TAGSHOTEL STATIONARYFERRY TICKETSP
HONECARDSMOVIE & THEATER TICKETSMENUSPA
SSPORT PHOTOSPARKING TICKETSTRAIN TICKETS
PHOTOGRAPHSRECIEPTSBEVERAGECOASTERSM
ATCHBOOKSLEAVESBROCHURESPAPER CURRENC
YSUBWAY TICKETSMUSEUM PASSESBUSINESS CA
RDSTOLLBOOTH RECIEPTSPRESSED FLOWERSCAN
DY WRAPPERSMAPSWINE LABELSLUGGAGE TAGS
HOTEL STATIONARYFERRY TICKETSPHONECARDS
MOVIE & THEATER TICKETSMENUSPASSPORT PHO
TOSPARKING TICKETSTRAIN TICKETSPHOTOGRAP
HSRECIEPTSBEVERAGECOASTERSMATCHBOOKSL
EAVESBROCHURESPAPER CURRENCYSUBWAY TIC
KETSMUSEUM PASSESBUSINESS CARDSTOLLBOO
TH RECIEPTSPRESSED FLOWERSCANDY WRAPPER
SMAPSWINE LABELSLUGGAGE TAGSHOTEL STATI
ONARYFERRY TICKETSPHONECARDSMOVIE & THE
ATER TICKETSMENUSPASSPORT PHOTOSPARKING
TICKETSTRAIN TICKETSPHOTOGRAPHSRECIEPTSB
EVERAGECOASTERSMATCHBOOKSLEAVESBROC
HURESPAPER CURRENCYSUBWAY TICKETSMUSEU
M PASSESBUSINESS CARDSTOLLBOOTH RECIEPTS
PRESSED FLOWERSCANDY WRAPPERSMAPSWINE
LABELSLUGGAGE TAGSHOTEL STATIONARYFERRY
TICKETSPHONECARDSMOVIE & THEATER TICKETS
MENUSPASSPORT PHOTOSPARKING TICKETSTRAI
N TICKETSPHOTOGRAPHSRECIEPTSBEVERAGECO
ASTERSMATCHBOOKSLEAVESBROCHURESPAPER
CURRENCYSUBWAY TICKETSMUSEUM PASSESBUS
INESS CARDSTOLLBOOTH RECIEPTSPRESSED FLO
WERSCANDY WRAPPERSMAPSWINE LABELSLUG
GAGE TAGSHOTEL STATIONARYFERRY TICKETSPH
ONECARDSMOVIE & THEATER TICKETSMENUSPAS
SPORT PHOTOSPARKING TICKETSTRAIN TICKETSP

PASTE HERE

DATE:

LOCATION:

LODGING:

TRANSPORTATION:

PLACES VISITED:

MEALS, RESTAURANTS, SPECIAL DISHES:

TRAIN TICKETSPHOTOGRAPHSRECIEPTSBEVERAGECOASTERSMATCHBOOKSLEAVESBROCHURESPAPER CURRENCYSUBWAY TICKETSMUSEUM PASSESBUSINESS CARDSTOLLBOOTH RECIEPTSPRESSED FLOWERSCANDY WRAPPERSMAPSWINE LABELSLUGGAGE TAGSHOTEL STATIONARYFERRY TICKETSPHONECARDSMOVIE & THEATER TICKETSMENUSPASSPORT PHOTOSPARKING TICKETSTRAIN TICKETSPHOTOGRAPHSRECIEPTSBEVERAGECOASTERSMATCHBOOKSLEAVESBROCHURESPAPER CURRENCYSUBWAY TICKETSMUSEUM PASSESBUSINESS CARDSTOLLBOOTH RECIEPTSPRESSED FLOWERSCANDY WRAPPERSMAPSWINE LABELSLUGGAGE TAGSHOTEL STATIONARYFERRY TICKETSPHONECARDSMOVIE & THEATER TICKETSMENUSPASSPORT PHOTOSPARKING TICKETSTRAIN TICKETSPHOTOGRAPHSRECIEPTSBEVERAGECOASTERSMATCHBOOKSLEAVESBROCHURESPAPER CURRENCYSUBWAY TICKETSMUSEUM PASSESBUSINESS CARDSTOLLBOOTH RECIEPTSPRESSED FLOWERSCANDY WRAPPERSMAPSWINE LABELSLUGGAGE TAGSHOTEL STATIONARYFERRY TICKETSPHONECARDSMOVIE & THEATER TICKETSMENUSPASSPORT PHOTOSPARKING TICKETSTRAIN TICKETSPHOTOGRAPHSRECIEPTSBEVERAGECOASTERSMATCHBOOKSLEAVESBROCHURESPAPER CURRENCYSUBWAY TICKETSMUSEUM PASSESBUSINESS CARDSTOLLBOOTH RECIEPTSPRESSED FLOWERSCANDY WRAPPERSMAPSWINE LABELSLUGGAGE TAGSHOTEL STATIONARYFERRY TICKETSPHONECARDSMOVIE & THEATER TICKETSMENUSPASSPORT PHOTOSPARKING TICKETSTRAIN TICKETSP

PASTE HERE

INTERESTING SHOPS:

ACQUISITIONS & GIFTS:

THINGS TOO LARGE, FRAGILE OR EXPENSIVE TO BUY:

NOTEWORTHY SIGHTS OR EXPERIENCES:

MEMORABLE ENCOUNTERS:

TRAIN TICKETSPHOTOGRAPHSRECIEPTSBEVERAG ECOASTERSMATCHBOOKSLEAVESBROCHURESPA PER CURRENCYSUBWAY TICKETSMUSEUM PASSES BUSINESS CARDSTOLLBOOTH RECIEPTSPRESSED F LOWERSCANDY WRAPPERSMAPSWINE LABELSLU GGAGE TAGSHOTEL STATIONARYFERRY TICKETSP HONECARDSMOVIE & THEATER TICKETSMENUSPA SSPORT PHOTOSPARKING TICKETSTRAIN TICKETS PHOTOGRAPHSRECIEPTSBEVERAGECOASTERSM ATCHBOOKSLEAVESBROCHURESPAPER CURRENC YSUBWAY TICKETSMUSEUM PASSESBUSINESS CA RDSTOLLBOOTH RECIEPTSPRESSED FLOWERSCAN DY WRAPPERSMAPSW̲I̲N̲E̲ ̲L̲ABELSLUGGAGE TAGS HOTEL STATIONARYF̲E̲R̲R̲Y̲ ̲T̲ICKETSPHONECARDS MOVIE & THEATER TIC̲K̲E̲T̲S̲MENUSPASSPORT PHO TOSPARKING TICKETST̲R̲A̲I̲N̲ TICKETSPHOTOGRAP HSRECIEPTSBEVERAGEC̲O̲A̲STERSMATCHBOOKSL EAVESBROCHURESPA̲P̲E̲R̲ ̲CURRENCYSUBWAY TIC KETSMUSEUM PASSE̲S̲B̲U̲S̲INESS CARDSTOLLBOO TH RECIEPTSPRESSED̲ ̲F̲L̲O̲WERSCANDY WRAPPER SMAPSWINE LABELSL̲U̲G̲G̲AGE TAGSHOTEL STATI ONARYFERRY TICKET̲S̲P̲H̲ONECARDSMOVIE & THE ATER TICKETSMENUS̲P̲A̲S̲SPORT PHOTOSPARKING TICKETSTRAIN TICKE̲T̲S̲P̲H̲OTOGRAPHSRECIEPTSB EVERAGECOASTERSMATCHBOOKSLEAVESBROC HURESPAPER CURRENCYSUBWAY TICKETSMUSEU M PASSESBUSINESS CARDSTOLLBOOTH RECIEPTS PRESSED FLOWERSCANDY WRAPPERSMAPSWINE LABELSLUGGAGE TAGSHOTEL STATIONARYFERRY TICKETSPHONECARDSMOVIE & THEATER TICKETS MENUSPASSPORT PHOTOSPARKING TICKETSTRAI N TICKETSPHOTOGRAPHSRECIEPTSBEVERAGECO ASTERSMATCHBOOKSLEAVESBROCHURESPAPER CURRENCYSUBWAY TICKETSMUSEUM PASSESBUS INESS CARDSTOLLBOOTH RECIEPTSPRESSED FLO WERSCANDY WRAPPERSMAPSWINE LABELSLUG GAGE TAGSHOTEL STATIONARYFERRY TICKETSPH ONECARDSMOVIE & THEATER TICKETSMENUSPA SPORT PHOTOSPARKING TICKETSTRAIN TICKETSP

PASTE HERE

DATE: _____

_____

LOCATION:
_____

_____

LODGING:
_____

_____

TRANSPORTATION:
_____

_____

_____

PLACES VISITED:
_____

_____

_____

_____

_____

_____

_____

MEALS, RESTAURANTS, SPECIAL DISHES:
_____

_____

_____

_____

_____

_____

_____

TRAIN TICKETSPHOTOGRAPHSRECIEPTSBEVERAG
ECOASTERSMATCHBOOKSLEAVESBROCHURESPA
PER CURRENCYSUBWAY TICKETSMUSEUM PASSES
BUSINESS CARDSTOLLBOOTH RECIEPTSPRESSED F
LOWERSCANDY WRAPPERSMAPSWINE LABELSLU
GGAGE TAGSHOTEL STATIONARYFERRY TICKETSP
HONECARDSMOVIE & THEATER TICKETSMENUSPA
SSPORT PHOTOSPARKING TICKETSTRAIN TICKETS
PHOTOGRAPHSRECIEPTSBEVERAGECOASTERSM
ATCHBOOKSLEAVESBROCHURESPAPER CURRENC
YSUBWAY TICKETSMUSEUM PASSESBUSINESS CA
RDSTOLLBOOTH RECIEPTSPRESSED FLOWERSCAN
DY WRAPPERSMAPSWINE LABELSLUGGAGE TAGS
HOTEL STATIONARYFERRY TICKETSPHONECARDS
MOVIE & THEATER TICKETSMENUSPASSPORT PHO
TOSPARKING TICKETSTRAIN TICKETSPHOTOGRAP
HSRECIEPTSBEVERAGECOASTERSMATCHBOOKSL
EAVESBROCHURESPAPER CURRENCYSUBWAY TIC
KETSMUSEUM PASSESBUSINESS CARDSTOLLBOO
TH RECIEPTSPRESSED FLOWERSCANDY WRAPPER
SMAPSWINE LABELSLUGGAGE TAGSHOTEL STATI
ONARYFERRY TICKETSPHONECARDSMOVIE & THE
ATER TICKETSMENUSPASSPORT PHOTOSPARKING
TICKETSTRAIN TICKETSPHOTOGRAPHSRECIEPTSB
EVERAGECOASTERSMATCHBOOKSLEAVESBROC
HURESPAPER CURRENCYSUBWAY TICKETSMUSEU
M PASSESBUSINESS CARDSTOLLBOOTH RECIEPTS
PRESSED FLOWERSCANDY WRAPPERSMAPSWINE
LABELSLUGGAGE TAGSHOTEL STATIONARYFERRY
TICKETSPHONECARDSMOVIE & THEATER TICKETS
MENUSPASSPORT PHOTOSPARKING TICKETSTRAI
N TICKETSPHOTOGRAPHSRECIEPTSBEVERAGECO
ASTERSMATCHBOOKSLEAVESBROCHURESPAPER
CURRENCYSUBWAY TICKETSMUSEUM PASSESBUS
INESS CARDSTOLLBOOTH RECIEPTSPRESSED FLO
WERSCANDY WRAPPERSMAPSWINE LABELSLUG
GAGE TAGSHOTEL STATIONARYFERRY TICKETSPH
ONECARDSMOVIE & THEATER TICKETSMENUSPAS
SPORT PHOTOSPARKING TICKETSTRAIN TICKETSP

PASTE HERE

INTERESTING SHOPS:

ACQUISITIONS & GIFTS:

THINGS TOO LARGE, FRAGILE OR EXPENSIVE TO BUY:

NOTEWORTHY SIGHTS OR EXPERIENCES:

MEMORABLE ENCOUNTERS:

TRAIN TICKETSPHOTOGRAPHSRECIEPTSBEVERAGECOASTERSMATCHBOOKSLEAVESBROCHURESPAPER CURRENCYSUBWAY TICKETSMUSEUM PASSESBUSINESS CARDSTOLLBOOTH RECIEPTSPRESSED FLOWERSCANDY WRAPPERSMAPSWINE LABELSLUGGAGE TAGSHOTEL STATIONARYFERRY TICKETSPHONECARDSMOVIE & THEATER TICKETSMENUSPASSPORT PHOTOSPARKING TICKETSTRAIN TICKETSPHOTOGRAPHSRECIEPTSBEVERAGECOASTERSMATCHBOOKSLEAVESBROCHURESPAPER CURRENCYSUBWAY TICKETSMUSEUM PASSESBUSINESS CARDSTOLLBOOTH RECIEPTSPRESSED FLOWERSCANDY WRAPPERSMAPSWINE LABELSLUGGAGE TAGSHOTEL STATIONARYFERRY TICKETSPHONECARDSMOVIE & THEATER TICKETSMENUSPASSPORT PHOTOSPARKING TICKETSTRAIN TICKETSPHOTOGRAPHSRECIEPTSBEVERAGECOASTERSMATCHBOOKSLEAVESBROCHURESPAPER CURRENCYSUBWAY TICKETSMUSEUM PASSESBUSINESS CARDSTOLLBOOTH RECIEPTSPRESSED FLOWERSCANDY WRAPPERSMAPSWINE LABELSLUGGAGE TAGSHOTEL STATIONARYFERRY TICKETSPHONECARDSMOVIE & THEATER TICKETSMENUSPASSPORT PHOTOSPARKING TICKETSTRAIN TICKETSPHOTOGRAPHSRECIEPTSBEVERAGECOASTERSMATCHBOOKSLEAVESBROCHURESPAPER CURRENCYSUBWAY TICKETSMUSEUM PASSESBUSINESS CARDSTOLLBOOTH RECIEPTSPRESSED FLOWERSCANDY WRAPPERSMAPSWINE LABELSLUGGAGE TAGSHOTEL STATIONARYFERRY TICKETSPHONECARDSMOVIE & THEATER TICKETSMENUSPASSPORT PHOTOSPARKING TICKETSTRAIN TICKETSPH

PASTE HERE

DATE:

DAY 6 DAY

LOCATION:

LODGING:

TRANSPORTATION:

PLACES VISITED:

MEALS, RESTAURANTS, SPECIAL DISHES:

TRAIN TICKETSPHOTOGRAPHSRECIEPTSBEVERAGECOASTERSMATCHBOOKSLEAVESBROCHURESPAPER CURRENCYSUBWAY TICKETSMUSEUM PASSESBUSINESS CARDSTOLLBOOTH RECIEPTSPRESSED FLOWERSCANDY WRAPPERSMAPSWINE LABELSLUGGAGE TAGSHOTEL STATIONARYFERRY TICKETSPHONECARDSMOVIE & THEATER TICKETSMENUSPASSPORT PHOTOSPARKING TICKETSTRAIN TICKETSPHOTOGRAPHSRECIEPTSBEVERAGECOASTERSMATCHBOOKSLEAVESBROCHURESPAPER CURRENCYSUBWAY TICKETSMUSEUM PASSESBUSINESS CARDSTOLLBOOTH RECIEPTSPRESSED FLOWERSCANDY WRAPPERSMAPSWINE LABELSLUGGAGE TAGSHOTEL STATIONARYFERRY TICKETSPHONECARDSMOVIE & THEATER TICKETSMENUSPASSPORT PHOTOSPARKING TICKETSTRAIN TICKETSPHOTOGRAPHSRECIEPTSBEVERAGECOASTERSMATCHBOOKSLEAVESBROCHURESPAPER CURRENCYSUBWAY TICKETSMUSEUM PASSESBUSINESS CARDSTOLLBOOTH RECIEPTSPRESSED FLOWERSCANDY WRAPPERSMAPSWINE LABELSLUGGAGE TAGSHOTEL STATIONARYFERRY TICKETSPHONECARDSMOVIE & THEATER TICKETSMENUSPASSPORT PHOTOSPARKING TICKETSTRAIN TICKETSPHOTOGRAPHSRECIEPTSBEVERAGECOASTERSMATCHBOOKSLEAVESBROCHURESPAPER CURRENCYSUBWAY TICKETSMUSEUM PASSESBUSINESS CARDSTOLLBOOTH RECIEPTSPRESSED FLOWERSCANDY WRAPPERSMAPSWINE LABELSLUGGAGE TAGSHOTEL STATIONARYFERRY TICKETSPHONECARDSMOVIE & THEATER TICKETSMENUSPASSPORT PHOTOSPARKING TICKETSTRAIN TICKETSPHOTOGRAPHSRECIEPTSBEVERAGECOASTERSMATCHBOOKSLEAVESBROCHURESPAPER CURRENCYSUBWAY TICKETSMUSEUM PASSESBUSINESS CARDSTOLLBOOTH RECIEPTSPRESSED FLOWERSCANDY WRAPPERSMAPSWINE LABELSLUGGAGE TAGSHOTEL STATIONARYFERRY TICKETSPHONECARDSMOVIE & THEATER TICKETSMENUSPAS SPORT PHOTOSPARKING TICKETSTRAIN TICKETSP

PASTE HERE

INTERESTING SHOPS:

ACQUISITIONS & GIFTS:

THINGS TOO LARGE, FRAGILE OR EXPENSIVE TO BUY:

NOTEWORTHY SIGHTS OR EXPERIENCES:

MEMORABLE ENCOUNTERS:

TRAIN TICKETSPHOTOGRAPHSRECIEPTSBEVERAG
ECOASTERSMATCHBOOKSLEAVESBROCHURESPA
PER CURRENCYSUBWAY TICKETSMUSEUM PASSES
BUSINESS CARDSTOLLBOOTH RECIEPTSPRESSED F
LOWERSCANDY WRAPPERSMAPSWINE LABELSLU
GGAGE TAGSHOTEL STATIONARYFERRY TICKETSP
HONECARDSMOVIE & THEATER TICKETSMENUSPA
SSPORT PHOTOSPARKING TICKETSTRAIN TICKETS
PHOTOGRAPHSRECIEPTSBEVERAGECOASTERSM
ATCHBOOKSLEAVESBROCHURESPAPER CURRENC
YSUBWAY TICKETSMUSEUM PASSESBUSINESS CA
RDSTOLLBOOTH RECIEPTSPRESSED FLOWERSCAN
DY WRAPPERSMAPSWINE LABELSLUGGAGE TAGS
HOTEL STATIONARYFERRY TICKETSPHONECARDS
MOVIE & THEATER TICKETSMENUSPASSPORT PHO
TOSPARKING TICKETSTRAIN TICKETSPHOTOGRAP
HSRECIEPTSBEVERAGECOASTERSMATCHBOOKSL
EAVESBROCHURESPAPER CURRENCYSUBWAY TIC
KETSMUSEUM PASSESBUSINESS CARDSTOLLBOO
TH RECIEPTSPRESSED FLOWERSCANDY WRAPPER
SMAPSWINE LABELSLUGGAGE TAGSHOTEL STATI
ONARYFERRY TICKETSPHONECARDSMOVIE & THE
ATER TICKETSMENUSPASSPORT PHOTOSPARKING
TICKETSTRAIN TICKETSPHOTOGRAPHSRECIEPTSB
EVERAGECOASTERSMATCHBOOKSLEAVESBROC
HURESPAPER CURRENCYSUBWAY TICKETSMUSEU
M PASSESBUSINESS CARDSTOLLBOOTH RECIEPTS
PRESSED FLOWERSCANDY WRAPPERSMAPSWINE
LABELSLUGGAGE TAGSHOTEL STATIONARYFERRY
TICKETSPHONECARDSMOVIE & THEATER TICKETS
MENUSPASSPORT PHOTOSPARKING TICKETSTRAI
N TICKETSPHOTOGRAPHSRECIEPTSBEVERAGECO
ASTERSMATCHBOOKSLEAVESBROCHURESPAPER
CURRENCYSUBWAY TICKETSMUSEUM PASSESBUS
INESS CARDSTOLLBOOTH RECIEPTSPRESSED FLO
WERSCANDY WRAPPERSMAPSWINE LABELSLUG
GAGE TAGSHOTEL STATIONARYFERRY TICKETSPH
ONECARDSMOVIE & THEATER TICKETSMENUSPAS
SPORT PHOTOSPARKING TICKETSTRAIN TICKETSP

PASTE HERE

DATE:

DAY 7 DAY

LOCATION:

LODGING:

TRANSPORTATION:

PLACES VISITED:

MEALS, RESTAURANTS, SPECIAL DISHES:

TRAIN TICKETSPHOTOGRAPHSRECIEPTSBEVERAG
ECOASTERSMATCHBOOKSLEAVESBROCHURESPA
PER CURRENCYSUBWAY TICKETSMUSEUM PASSES
BUSINESS CARDSTOLLBOOTH RECIEPTSPRESSED F
LOWERSCANDY WRAPPERSMAPSWINE LABELSLU
GGAGE TAGSHOTEL STATIONARYFERRY TICKETSP
HONECARDSMOVIE & THEATER TICKETSMENUSPA
SSPORT PHOTOSPARKING TICKETSTRAIN TICKETS
PHOTOGRAPHSRECIEPTSBEVERAGECOASTERSM
ATCHBOOKSLEAVESBROCHURESPAPER CURRENC
YSUBWAY TICKETSMUSEUM PASSESBUSINESS CA
RDSTOLLBOOTH RECIEPTSPRESSED FLOWERSCAN
DY WRAPPERSMAPSWINE LABELSLUGGAGE TAGS
HOTEL STATIONARYFERRY TICKETSPHONECARDS
MOVIE & THEATER TICKETSMENUSPASSPORT PHO
TOSPARKING TICKETSTRAIN TICKETSPHOTOGRAP
HSRECIEPTSBEVERAGECOASTERSMATCHBOOKSL
EAVESBROCHURESPAPER CURRENCYSUBWAY TIC
KETSMUSEUM PASSESBUSINESS CARDSTOLLBOO
TH RECIEPTSPRESSED FLOWERSCANDY WRAPPER
SMAPSWINE LABELSLUGGAGE TAGSHOTEL STATI
ONARYFERRY TICKETSPHONECARDSMOVIE & THE
ATER TICKETSMENUSPASSPORT PHOTOSPARKING
TICKETSTRAIN TICKETSPHOTOGRAPHSRECIEPTSB
EVERAGECOASTERSMATCHBOOKSLEAVESBROC
HURESPAPER CURRENCYSUBWAY TICKETSMUSEU
M PASSESBUSINESS CARDSTOLLBOOTH RECIEPTS
PRESSED FLOWERSCANDY WRAPPERSMAPSWINE
LABELSLUGGAGE TAGSHOTEL STATIONARYFERRY
TICKETSPHONECARDSMOVIE & THEATER TICKETS
MENUSPASSPORT PHOTOSPARKING TICKETSTRAI
N TICKETSPHOTOGRAPHSRECIEPTSBEVERAGECO
ASTERSMATCHBOOKSLEAVESBROCHURESPAPER
CURRENCYSUBWAY TICKETSMUSEUM PASSESBUS
INESS CARDSTOLLBOOTH RECIEPTSPRESSED FLO
WERSCANDY WRAPPERSMAPSWINE LABELSLUG
GAGE TAGSHOTEL STATIONARYFERRY TICKETSPH
ONECARDSMOVIE & THEATER TICKETSMENUSPAS
SPORT PHOTOSPARKING TICKETSTRAIN TICKETSP

PASTE HERE

INTERESTING SHOPS:

ACQUISITIONS & GIFTS:

THINGS TOO LARGE, FRAGILE OR EXPENSIVE TO BUY:

NOTEWORTHY SIGHTS OR EXPERIENCES:

MEMORABLE ENCOUNTERS:

WEEK

TRAIN TICKETSPHOTOGRAPHSRECIEPTSBEVERAG
ECOASTERSMATCHBOOKSLEAVESBROCHURESPA
PER CURRENCYSUBWAY TICKETSMUSEUM PASSES
BUSINESS CARDSTOLLBOOTH RECIEPTSPRESSED F
LOWERSCANDY WRAPPERSMAPSWINE LABELSLU
GGAGE TAGSHOTEL STATIONARYFERRY TICKETSP
HONECARDSMOVIE & THEATER TICKETSMENUSPA
SSPORT PHOTOSPARKING TICKETSTRAIN TICKETS
PHOTOGRAPHSRECIEPTSBEVERAGECOASTERSM
ATCHBOOKSLEAVESBROCHURESPAPER CURRENC
YSUBWAY TICKETSMUSEUM PASSESBUSINESS CA
RDSTOLLBOOTH RECIEPTSPRESSED FLOWERSCAN
DY WRAPPERSMAPSWINE LABELSLUGGAGE TAGS
HOTEL STATIONARYFERRY TICKETSPHONECARDS
MOVIE & THEATER TICKETSMENUSPASSPORT PHO
TOSPARKING TICKETSTRAIN TICKETSPHOTOGRAP
HSRECIEPTSBEVERAGECOASTERSMATCHBOOKSL
EAVESBROCHURESPAPER CURRENCYSUBWAY TIC
KETSMUSEUM PASSESBUSINESS CARDSTOLLBOO
TH RECIEPTSPRESSED FLOWERSCANDY WRAPPER
SMAPSWINE LABELSLUGGAGE TAGSHOTEL STATI
ONARYFERRY TICKETSPHONECARDSMOVIE & THE
ATER TICKETSMENUSPASSPORT PHOTOSPARKING
TICKETSTRAIN TICKETSPHOTOGRAPHSRECIEPTSB
EVERAGECOASTERSMATCHBOOKSLEAVESBROC
HURESPAPER CURRENCYSUBWAY TICKETSMUSEU
M PASSESBUSINESS CARDSTOLLBOOTH RECIEPTS
PRESSED FLOWERSCANDY WRAPPERSMAPSWINE
LABELSLUGGAGE TAGSHOTEL STATIONARYFERRY
TICKETSPHONECARDSMOVIE & THEATER TICKETS
MENUSPASSPORT PHOTOSPARKING TICKETSTRAI
N TICKETSPHOTOGRAPHSRECIEPTSBEVERAGECO
ASTERSMATCHBOOKSLEAVESBROCHURESPAPER
CURRENCYSUBWAY TICKETSMUSEUM PASSESBUS
INESS CARDSTOLLBOOTH RECIEPTSPRESSED FLO
WERSCANDY WRAPPERSMAPSWINE LABELSLUG
GAGE TAGSHOTEL STATIONARYFERRY TICKETSPH
ONECARDSMOVIE & THEATER TICKETSMENUSPAS
SPORT PHOTOSPARKING TICKETSTRAIN TICKETSP

PASTE HERE

DATE:

LOCATION:

LODGING:

TRANSPORTATION:

PLACES VISITED:

MEALS, RESTAURANTS, SPECIAL DISHES:

TRAIN TICKETSPHOTOGRAPHSRECIEPTSBEVERAG
ECOASTERSMATCHBOOKSLEAVESBROCHURESPA
PER CURRENCYSUBWAY TICKETSMUSEUM PASSES
BUSINESS CARDSTOLLBOOTH RECIEPTSPRESSED F
LOWERSCANDY WRAPPERSMAPSWINE LABELSLU
GGAGE TAGSHOTEL STATIONARYFERRY TICKETSP
HONECARDSMOVIE & THEATER TICKETSMENUSPA
SSPORT PHOTOSPARKING TICKETSTRAIN TICKETS
PHOTOGRAPHSRECIEPTSBEVERAGECOASTERSM
ATCHBOOKSLEAVESBROCHURESPAPER CURRENC
YSUBWAY TICKETSMUSEUM PASSESBUSINESS CA
RDSTOLLBOOTH RECIEPTSPRESSED FLOWERSCAN
DY WRAPPERSMAPSWINE LABELSLUGGAGE TAGS
HOTEL STATIONARYFERRY TICKETSPHONECARDS
MOVIE & THEATER TICKETSMENUSPASSPORT PHO
TOSPARKING TICKETSTRAIN TICKETSPHOTOGRAP
HSRECIEPTSBEVERAGECOASTERSMATCHBOOKSL
EAVESBROCHURESPAPER CURRENCYSUBWAY TIC
KETSMUSEUM PASSESBUSINESS CARDSTOLLBOO
TH RECIEPTSPRESSED FLOWERSCANDY WRAPPER
SMAPSWINE LABELSLUGGAGE TAGSHOTEL STATI
ONARYFERRY TICKETSPHONECARDSMOVIE & THE
ATER TICKETSMENUSPASSPORT PHOTOSPARKING
TICKETSTRAIN TICKETSPHOTOGRAPHSRECIEPTSB
EVERAGECOASTERSMATCHBOOKSLEAVESBROC
HURESPAPER CURRENCYSUBWAY TICKETSMUSEU
M PASSESBUSINESS CARDSTOLLBOOTH RECIEPTS
PRESSED FLOWERSCANDY WRAPPERSMAPSWINE
LABELSLUGGAGE TAGSHOTEL STATIONARYFERRY
TICKETSPHONECARDSMOVIE & THEATER TICKETS
MENUSPASSPORT PHOTOSPARKING TICKETSTRAI
N TICKETSPHOTOGRAPHSRECIEPTSBEVERAGECO
ASTERSMATCHBOOKSLEAVESBROCHURESPAPER
CURRENCYSUBWAY TICKETSMUSEUM PASSESBUS
INESS CARDSTOLLBOOTH RECIEPTSPRESSED FLO
WERSCANDY WRAPPERSMAPSWINE LABELSLUG
GAGE TAGSHOTEL STATIONARYFERRY TICKETSPH
ONECARDSMOVIE & THEATER TICKETSMENUSPAS
SPORT PHOTOSPARKING TICKETSTRAIN TICKETSP

PASTE HERE

INTERESTING SHOPS:

ACQUISITIONS & GIFTS:

THINGS TOO LARGE, FRAGILE OR EXPENSIVE TO BUY:

NOTEWORTHY SIGHTS OR EXPERIENCES:

MEMORABLE ENCOUNTERS:

TRAIN TICKETSPHOTOGRAPHSRECIEPTSBEVERAG
ECOASTERSMATCHBOOKSLEAVESBROCHURESPA
PER CURRENCYSUBWAY TICKETSMUSEUM PASSES
BUSINESS CARDSTOLLBOOTH RECIEPTSPRESSED F
LOWERSCANDY WRAPPERSMAPSWINE LABELSLU
GGAGE TAGSHOTEL STATIONARYFERRY TICKETSP
HONECARDSMOVIE & THEATER TICKETSMENUSPA
SSPORT PHOTOSPARKING TICKETSTRAIN TICKETS
PHOTOGRAPHSRECIEPTSBEVERAGECOASTERSM
ATCHBOOKSLEAVESBROCHURESPAPER CURRENC
YSUBWAY TICKETSMUSEUM PASSESBUSINESS CA
RDSTOLLBOOTH RECIEPTSPRESSED FLOWERSCAN
DY WRAPPERSMAPSW**P**INE LABELSLUGGAGE TAGS
HOTEL STATIONARYFE**A**RRY TICKETSPHONECARDS
MOVIE & THEATER TIC**S**KETSMENUSPASSPORT PHO
TOSPARKING TICKETS**T**TRAIN TICKETSPHOTOGRAP
HSRECIEPTSBEVERAG**E**ECOASTERSMATCHBOOKSL
EAVESBROCHURESPA**H**URRENCYSUBWAY TIC
KETSMUSEUM PASSE**E**SBUSINESS CARDSTOLLBOO
TH RECIEPTSPRESSED**R**FLOWERSCANDY WRAPPER
SMAPSWINE LABELSL**E**UGGAGE TAGSHOTEL STATI
ONARYFERRY TICKETS PHONECARDSMOVIE & THE
ATER TICKETSMENUSPASSPORT PHOTOSPARKING
TICKETSTRAIN TICKETSPHOTOGRAPHSRECIEPTSB
EVERAGECOASTERSMATCHBOOKSLEAVESBROC
HURESPAPER CURRENCYSUBWAY TICKETSMUSEU
M PASSESBUSINESS CARDSTOLLBOOTH RECIEPTS
PRESSED FLOWERSCANDY WRAPPERSMAPSWINE
LABELSLUGGAGE TAGSHOTEL STATIONARYFERRY
TICKETSPHONECARDSMOVIE & THEATER TICKETS
MENUSPASSPORT PHOTOSPARKING TICKETSTRAI
N TICKETSPHOTOGRAPHSRECIEPTSBEVERAGECO
ASTERSMATCHBOOKSLEAVESBROCHURESPAPER
CURRENCYSUBWAY TICKETSMUSEUM PASSESBUS
INESS CARDSTOLLBOOTH RECIEPTSPRESSED FLO
WERSCANDY WRAPPERSMAPSWINE LABELSLUG
GAGE TAGSHOTEL STATIONARYFERRY TICKETSPH
ONECARDSMOVIE & THEATER TICKETSMENUSPAS
SPORT PHOTOSPARKING TICKETSTRAIN TICKETSB

PASTE HERE

DATE:

DAY 9 DAY

LOCATION:

LODGING:

TRANSPORTATION:

PLACES VISITED:

MEALS, RESTAURANTS, SPECIAL DISHES:

TRAIN TICKETSPHOTOGRAPHSRECIEPTSBEVERAGECOASTERSMATCHBOOKSLEAVESBROCHURESPAPER CURRENCYSUBWAY TICKETSMUSEUM PASSESBUSINESS CARDSTOLLBOOTH RECIEPTSPRESSED FLOWERSCANDY WRAPPERSMAPSWINE LABELSLUGGAGE TAGSHOTEL STATIONARYFERRY TICKETSPHONECARDSMOVIE & THEATER TICKETSMENUSPASSPORT PHOTOSPARKING TICKETSTRAIN TICKETSPHOTOGRAPHSRECIEPTSBEVERAGECOASTERSMATCHBOOKSLEAVESBROCHURESPAPER CURRENCYSUBWAY TICKETSMUSEUM PASSESBUSINESS CARDSTOLLBOOTH RECIEPTSPRESSED FLOWERSCANDY WRAPPERSMAPSWINE LABELSLUGGAGE TAGSHOTEL STATIONARYFERRY TICKETSPHONECARDSMOVIE & THEATER TICKETSMENUSPASSPORT PHOTOSPARKING TICKETSTRAIN TICKETSPHOTOGRAPHSRECIEPTSBEVERAGECOASTERSMATCHBOOKSLEAVESBROCHURESPAPER CURRENCYSUBWAY TICKETSMUSEUM PASSESBUSINESS CARDSTOLLBOOTH RECIEPTSPRESSED FLOWERSCANDY WRAPPERSMAPSWINE LABELSLUGGAGE TAGSHOTEL STATIONARYFERRY TICKETSPHONECARDSMOVIE & THEATER TICKETSMENUSPASSPORT PHOTOSPARKING TICKETSTRAIN TICKETSPHOTOGRAPHSRECIEPTSBEVERAGECOASTERSMATCHBOOKSLEAVESBROCHURESPAPER CURRENCYSUBWAY TICKETSMUSEUM PASSESBUSINESS CARDSTOLLBOOTH RECIEPTSPRESSED FLOWERSCANDY WRAPPERSMAPSWINE LABELSLUGGAGE TAGSHOTEL STATIONARYFERRY TICKETSPHONECARDSMOVIE & THEATER TICKETSMENUSPASSPORT PHOTOSPARKING TICKETSTRAIN TICKETSPHOTOGRAPHSRECIEPTSBEVERAGECOASTERSMATCHBOOKSLEAVESBROCHURESPAPER CURRENCYSUBWAY TICKETSMUSEUM PASSESBUSINESS CARDSTOLLBOOTH RECIEPTSPRESSED FLOWERSCANDY WRAPPERSMAPSWINE LABELSLUGGAGE TAGSHOTEL STATIONARYFERRY TICKETSPHONECARDSMOVIE & THEATER TICKETSMENUSPASSPORT PHOTOSPARKING TICKETSTRAIN TICKETSP

PASTE HERE

DAY 9 DAY

INTERESTING SHOPS:

ACQUISITIONS & GIFTS:

THINGS TOO LARGE, FRAGILE OR EXPENSIVE TO BUY:

NOTEWORTHY SIGHTS OR EXPERIENCES:

MEMORABLE ENCOUNTERS:

TRAIN TICKETSPHOTOGRAPHSRECIEPTSBEVERAG
ECOASTERSMATCHBOOKSLEAVESBROCHURESPA
PER CURRENCYSUBWAY TICKETSMUSEUM PASSES
BUSINESS CARDSTOLLBOOTH RECIEPTSPRESSED F
LOWERSCANDY WRAPPERSMAPSWINE LABELSLU
GGAGE TAGSHOTEL STATIONARYFERRY TICKETSP
HONECARDSMOVIE & THEATER TICKETSMENUSPA
SSPORT PHOTOSPARKING TICKETSTRAIN TICKETS
PHOTOGRAPHSRECIEPTSBEVERAGECOASTERSM
ATCHBOOKSLEAVESBROCHURESPAPER CURRENC
YSUBWAY TICKETSMUSEUM PASSESBUSINESS CA
RDSTOLLBOOTH RECIEPTSPRESSED FLOWERSCAN
DY WRAPPERSMAPSWINE LABELSLUGGAGE TAGS
HOTEL STATIONARYFERRY TICKETSPHONECARDS
MOVIE & THEATER TICKETSMENUSPASSPORT PHO
TOSPARKING TICKETSTRAIN TICKETSPHOTOGRAP
HSRECIEPTSBEVERAGECOASTERSMATCHBOOKSL
EAVESBROCHURESPAPER CURRENCYSUBWAY TIC
KETSMUSEUM PASSESBUSINESS CARDSTOLLBOO
TH RECIEPTSPRESSED FLOWERSCANDY WRAPPER
SMAPSWINE LABELSLUGGAGE TAGSHOTEL STATI
ONARYFERRY TICKETSPHONECARDSMOVIE & THE
ATER TICKETSMENUSPASSPORT PHOTOSPARKING
TICKETSTRAIN TICKETSPHOTOGRAPHSRECIEPTSB
EVERAGECOASTERSMATCHBOOKSLEAVESBROC
HURESPAPER CURRENCYSUBWAY TICKETSMUSEU
M PASSESBUSINESS CARDSTOLLBOOTH RECIEPTS
PRESSED FLOWERSCANDY WRAPPERSMAPSWINE
LABELSLUGGAGE TAGSHOTEL STATIONARYFERRY
TICKETSPHONECARDSMOVIE & THEATER TICKETS
MENUSPASSPORT PHOTOSPARKING TICKETSTRAI
N TICKETSPHOTOGRAPHSRECIEPTSBEVERAGECO
ASTERSMATCHBOOKSLEAVESBROCHURESPAPER
CURRENCYSUBWAY TICKETSMUSEUM PASSESBUS
INESS CARDSTOLLBOOTH RECIEPTSPRESSED FLO
WERSCANDY WRAPPERSMAPSWINE LABELSLUG
GAGE TAGSHOTEL STATIONARYFERRY TICKETSPH
ONECARDSMOVIE & THEATER TICKETSMENUSPAS
SPORT PHOTOSPARKING TICKETSTRAIN TICKETSP

PASTE HERE

DATE:

LOCATION:

LODGING:

TRANSPORTATION:

PLACES VISITED:

MEALS, RESTAURANTS, SPECIAL DISHES:

TRAIN TICKETSPHOTOGRAPHSRECIEPTSBEVERAG
ECOASTERSMATCHBOOKSLEAVESBROCHURESPA
PER CURRENCYSUBWAY TICKETSMUSEUM PASSES
BUSINESS CARDSTOLLBOOTH RECIEPTSPRESSED F
LOWERSCANDY WRAPPERSMAPSWINE LABELSLU
GGAGE TAGSHOTEL STATIONARYFERRY TICKETSP
HONECARDSMOVIE & THEATER TICKETSMENUSPA
SSPORT PHOTOSPARKING TICKETSTRAIN TICKETS
PHOTOGRAPHSRECIEPTSBEVERAGECOASTERSM
ATCHBOOKSLEAVESBROCHURESPAPER CURRENC
YSUBWAY TICKETSMUSEUM PASSESBUSINESS CA
RDSTOLLBOOTH RECIEPTSPRESSED FLOWERSCAN
DY WRAPPERSMAPSWINE LABELSLUGGAGE TAGS
HOTEL STATIONARYFERRY TICKETSPHONECARDS
MOVIE & THEATER TICKETSMENUSPASSPORT PHO
TOSPARKING TICKETSTRAIN TICKETSPHOTOGRAP
HSRECIEPTSBEVERAGECOASTERSMATCHBOOKSL
EAVESBROCHURESPAPER CURRENCYSUBWAY TIC
KETSMUSEUM PASSESBUSINESS CARDSTOLLBOO
TH RECIEPTSPRESSED FLOWERSCANDY WRAPPER
SMAPSWINE LABELSLUGGAGE TAGSHOTEL STATI
ONARYFERRY TICKETSPHONECARDSMOVIE & THE
ATER TICKETSMENUSPASSPORT PHOTOSPARKING
TICKETSTRAIN TICKETSPHOTOGRAPHSRECIEPTSB
EVERAGECOASTERSMATCHBOOKSLEAVESBROC
HURESPAPER CURRENCYSUBWAY TICKETSMUSEU
M PASSESBUSINESS CARDSTOLLBOOTH RECIEPTS
PRESSED FLOWERSCANDY WRAPPERSMAPSWINE
LABELSLUGGAGE TAGSHOTEL STATIONARYFERRY
TICKETSPHONECARDSMOVIE & THEATER TICKETS
MENUSPASSPORT PHOTOSPARKING TICKETSTRAI
N TICKETSPHOTOGRAPHSRECIEPTSBEVERAGECO
ASTERSMATCHBOOKSLEAVESBROCHURESPAPER
CURRENCYSUBWAY TICKETSMUSEUM PASSESBUS
INESS CARDSTOLLBOOTH RECIEPTSPRESSED FLO
WERSCANDY WRAPPERSMAPSWINE LABELSLUG
GAGE TAGSHOTEL STATIONARYFERRY TICKETSPH
ONECARDSMOVIE & THEATER TICKETSMENUSPAS
SPORT PHOTOSPARKING TICKETSTRAIN TICKETSP

PASTE HERE

INTERESTING SHOPS:

ACQUISITIONS & GIFTS:

THINGS TOO LARGE, FRAGILE OR EXPENSIVE TO BUY:

NOTEWORTHY SIGHTS OR EXPERIENCES:

MEMORABLE ENCOUNTERS:

TRAIN TICKETSPHOTOGRAPHSRECIEPTSBEVERAG
ECOASTERSMATCHBOOKSLEAVESBROCHURESPA
PER CURRENCYSUBWAY TICKETSMUSEUM PASSES
BUSINESS CARDSTOLLBOOTH RECIEPTSPRESSED F
LOWERSCANDY WRAPPERSMAPSWINE LABELSLU
GGAGE TAGSHOTEL STATIONARYFERRY TICKETSP
HONECARDSMOVIE & THEATER TICKETSMENUSPA
SSPORT PHOTOSPARKING TICKETSTRAIN TICKETS
PHOTOGRAPHSRECIEPTSBEVERAGECOASTERSM
ATCHBOOKSLEAVESBROCHURESPAPER CURRENC
YSUBWAY TICKETSMUSEUM PASSESBUSINESS CA
RDSTOLLBOOTH RECIEPTSPRESSED FLOWERSCAN
DY WRAPPERSMAPSWINE LABELSLUGGAGE TAGS
HOTEL STATIONARYFERRY TICKETSPHONECARDS
MOVIE & THEATER TICKETSMENUSPASSPORT PHO
TOSPARKING TICKETSTRAIN TICKETSPHOTOGRAP
HSRECIEPTSBEVERAGECOASTERSMATCHBOOKSL
EAVESBROCHURESPAPER CURRENCYSUBWAY TIC
KETSMUSEUM PASSESBUSINESS CARDSTOLLBOO
TH RECIEPTSPRESSED FLOWERSCANDY WRAPPER
SMAPSWINE LABELSLUGGAGE TAGSHOTEL STATI
ONARYFERRY TICKETSPHONECARDSMOVIE & THE
ATER TICKETSMENUSPASSPORT PHOTOSPARKING
TICKETSTRAIN TICKETSPHOTOGRAPHSRECIEPTSB
EVERAGECOASTERSMATCHBOOKSLEAVESBROC
HURESPAPER CURRENCYSUBWAY TICKETSMUSEU
M PASSESBUSINESS CARDSTOLLBOOTH RECIEPTS
PRESSED FLOWERSCANDY WRAPPERSMAPSWINE
LABELSLUGGAGE TAGSHOTEL STATIONARYFERRY
TICKETSPHONECARDSMOVIE & THEATER TICKETS
MENUSPASSPORT PHOTOSPARKING TICKETSTRAI
N TICKETSPHOTOGRAPHSRECIEPTSBEVERAGECO
ASTERSMATCHBOOKSLEAVESBROCHURESPAPER
CURRENCYSUBWAY TICKETSMUSEUM PASSESBUS
INESS CARDSTOLLBOOTH RECIEPTSPRESSED FLO
WERSCANDY WRAPPERSMAPSWINE LABELSLUG
GAGE TAGSHOTEL STATIONARYFERRY TICKETSPH
ONECARDSMOVIE & THEATER TICKETSMENUSPAS
SPORT PHOTOSPARKING TICKETSTRAIN TICKETSP

PASTE HERE

DATE:

D A Y   D A Y

LOCATION:

_____

LODGING:

_____

TRANSPORTATION:

_____

_____

PLACES VISITED:

_____

_____

_____

_____

_____

_____

_____

MEALS, RESTAURANTS, SPECIAL DISHES:

_____

_____

_____

_____

_____

_____

_____

TRAIN TICKETSPHOTOGRAPHSRECIEPTSBEVERAG
ECOASTERSMATCHBOOKSLEAVESBROCHURESPA
PER CURRENCYSUBWAY TICKETSMUSEUM PASSES
BUSINESS CARDSTOLLBOOTH RECIEPTSPRESSED F
LOWERSCANDY WRAPPERSMAPSWINE LABELSLU
GGAGE TAGSHOTEL STATIONARYFERRY TICKETSP
HONECARDSMOVIE & THEATER TICKETSMENUSPA
SSPORT PHOTOSPARKING TICKETSTRAIN TICKETS
PHOTOGRAPHSRECIEPTSBEVERAGECOASTERSM
ATCHBOOKSLEAVESBROCHURESPAPER CURRENC
YSUBWAY TICKETSMUSEUM PASSESBUSINESS CA
RDSTOLLBOOTH RECIEPTSPRESSED FLOWERSCAN
DY WRAPPERSMAPSWINE LABELSLUGGAGE TAGS
HOTEL STATIONARYFERRY TICKETSPHONECARDS
MOVIE & THEATER TICKETSMENUSPASSPORT PHO
TOSPARKING TICKETSTRAIN TICKETSPHOTOGRAP
HSRECIEPTSBEVERAGECOASTERSMATCHBOOKSL
EAVESBROCHURESPAPER CURRENCYSUBWAY TIC
KETSMUSEUM PASSESBUSINESS CARDSTOLLBOO
TH RECIEPTSPRESSED FLOWERSCANDY WRAPPER
SMAPSWINE LABELSLUGGAGE TAGSHOTEL STATI
ONARYFERRY TICKETSPHONECARDSMOVIE & THE
ATER TICKETSMENUSPASSPORT PHOTOSPARKING
TICKETSTRAIN TICKETSPHOTOGRAPHSRECIEPTSB
EVERAGECOASTERSMATCHBOOKSLEAVESBROC
HURESPAPER CURRENCYSUBWAY TICKETSMUSEU
M PASSESBUSINESS CARDSTOLLBOOTH RECIEPTS
PRESSED FLOWERSCANDY WRAPPERSMAPSWINE
LABELSLUGGAGE TAGSHOTEL STATIONARYFERRY
TICKETSPHONECARDSMOVIE & THEATER TICKETS
MENUSPASSPORT PHOTOSPARKING TICKETSTRAI
N TICKETSPHOTOGRAPHSRECIEPTSBEVERAGECO
ASTERSMATCHBOOKSLEAVESBROCHURESPAPER
CURRENCYSUBWAY TICKETSMUSEUM PASSESBUS
INESS CARDSTOLLBOOTH RECIEPTSPRESSED FLO
WERSCANDY WRAPPERSMAPSWINE LABELSLUG
GAGE TAGSHOTEL STATIONARYFERRY TICKETSPH
ONECARDSMOVIE & THEATER TICKETSMENUSPAS
SPORT PHOTOSPARKING TICKETSTRAIN TICKETSP

PASTE HERE

INTERESTING SHOPS:

ACQUISITIONS & GIFTS:

THINGS TOO LARGE, FRAGILE OR EXPENSIVE TO BUY:

NOTEWORTHY SIGHTS OR EXPERIENCES:

MEMORABLE ENCOUNTERS:

TRAIN TICKETSPHOTOGRAPHSRECIEPTSBEVERAG
ECOASTERSMATCHBOOKSLEAVESBROCHURESPA
PER CURRENCYSUBWAY TICKETSMUSEUM PASSES
BUSINESS CARDSTOLLBOOTH RECIEPTSPRESSED F
LOWERSCANDY WRAPPERSMAPSWINE LABELSLU
GGAGE TAGSHOTEL STATIONARYFERRY TICKETSP
HONECARDSMOVIE & THEATER TICKETSMENUSPA
SSPORT PHOTOSPARKING TICKETSTRAIN TICKETS
PHOTOGRAPHSRECIEPTSBEVERAGECOASTERSM
ATCHBOOKSLEAVESBROCHURESPAPER CURRENC
YSUBWAY TICKETSMUSEUM PASSESBUSINESS CA
RDSTOLLBOOTH RECIEPTSPRESSED FLOWERSCAN
DY WRAPPERSMAPSWINE LABELSLUGGAGE TAGS
HOTEL STATIONARYFERRY TICKETSPHONECARDS
MOVIE & THEATER TICKETSMENUSPASSPORT PHO
TOSPARKING TICKETSTRAIN TICKETSPHOTOGRAP
HSRECIEPTSBEVERAGECOASTERSMATCHBOOKSL
EAVESBROCHURESPAPER CURRENCYSUBWAY TIC
KETSMUSEUM PASSESBUSINESS CARDSTOLLBOO
TH RECIEPTSPRESSED FLOWERSCANDY WRAPPER
SMAPSWINE LABELSLUGGAGE TAGSHOTEL STATI
ONARYFERRY TICKETSPHONECARDSMOVIE & THE
ATER TICKETSMENUSPASSPORT PHOTOSPARKING
TICKETSTRAIN TICKETSPHOTOGRAPHSRECIEPTSB
EVERAGECOASTERSMATCHBOOKSLEAVESBROC
HURESPAPER CURRENCYSUBWAY TICKETSMUSEU
M PASSESBUSINESS CARDSTOLLBOOTH RECIEPTS
PRESSED FLOWERSCANDY WRAPPERSMAPSWINE
LABELSLUGGAGE TAGSHOTEL STATIONARYFERRY
TICKETSPHONECARDSMOVIE & THEATER TICKETS
MENUSPASSPORT PHOTOSPARKING TICKETSTRAI
N TICKETSPHOTOGRAPHSRECIEPTSBEVERAGECO
ASTERSMATCHBOOKSLEAVESBROCHURESPAPER
CURRENCYSUBWAY TICKETSMUSEUM PASSESBUS
INESS CARDSTOLLBOOTH RECIEPTSPRESSED FLO
WERSCANDY WRAPPERSMAPSWINE LABELSLUG
GAGE TAGSHOTEL STATIONARYFERRY TICKETSPH
ONECARDSMOVIE & THEATER TICKETSMENUSPAS
SPORT PHOTOSPARKING TICKETSTRAIN TICKETSP

PASTE HERE

DATE: _____

_____

LOCATION:

_____

_____

LODGING:

_____

_____

TRANSPORTATION:

_____

_____

_____

PLACES VISITED:

_____

_____

_____

_____

_____

_____

_____

_____

MEALS, RESTAURANTS, SPECIAL DISHES:

_____

_____

_____

_____

_____

_____

_____

TRAIN TICKETSPHOTOGRAPHSRECIEPTSBEVERAG
ECOASTERSMATCHBOOKSLEAVESBROCHURESPA
PER CURRENCYSUBWAY TICKETSMUSEUM PASSES
BUSINESS CARDSTOLLBOOTH RECIEPTSPRESSED F
LOWERSCANDY WRAPPERSMAPSWINE LABELSLU
GGAGE TAGSHOTEL STATIONARYFERRY TICKETSP
HONECARDSMOVIE & THEATER TICKETSMENUSPA
SSPORT PHOTOSPARKING TICKETSTRAIN TICKETS
PHOTOGRAPHSRECIEPTSBEVERAGECOASTERSM
ATCHBOOKSLEAVESBROCHURESPAPER CURRENC
YSUBWAY TICKETSMUSEUM PASSESBUSINESS CA
RDSTOLLBOOTH RECIEPTSPRESSED FLOWERSCAN
DY WRAPPERSMAPSWINE LABELSLUGGAGE TAGS
HOTEL STATIONARYFERRY TICKETSPHONECARDS
MOVIE & THEATER TICKETSMENUSPASSPORT PHO
TOSPARKING TICKETSTRAIN TICKETSPHOTOGRAP
HSRECIEPTSBEVERAGECOASTERSMATCHBOOKSL
EAVESBROCHURESPAPER CURRENCYSUBWAY TIC
KETSMUSEUM PASSESBUSINESS CARDSTOLLBOO
TH RECIEPTSPRESSED FLOWERSCANDY WRAPPER
SMAPSWINE LABELSLUGGAGE TAGSHOTEL STATI
ONARYFERRY TICKETSPHONECARDSMOVIE & THE
ATER TICKETSMENUSPASSPORT PHOTOSPARKING
TICKETSTRAIN TICKETSPHOTOGRAPHSRECIEPTSB
EVERAGECOASTERSMATCHBOOKSLEAVESBROC
HURESPAPER CURRENCYSUBWAY TICKETSMUSEU
M PASSESBUSINESS CARDSTOLLBOOTH RECIEPTS
PRESSED FLOWERSCANDY WRAPPERSMAPSWINE
LABELSLUGGAGE TAGSHOTEL STATIONARYFERRY
TICKETSPHONECARDSMOVIE & THEATER TICKETS
MENUSPASSPORT PHOTOSPARKING TICKETSTRAI
N TICKETSPHOTOGRAPHSRECIEPTSBEVERAGECO
ASTERSMATCHBOOKSLEAVESBROCHURESPAPER
CURRENCYSUBWAY TICKETSMUSEUM PASSESBUS
INESS CARDSTOLLBOOTH RECIEPTSPRESSED FLO
WERSCANDY WRAPPERSMAPSWINE LABELSLUG
GAGE TAGSHOTEL STATIONARYFERRY TICKETSPH
ONECARDSMOVIE & THEATER TICKETSMENUSPAS
SPORT PHOTOSPARKING TICKETSTRAIN TICKETSP

PASTE HERE

INTERESTING SHOPS:

ACQUISITIONS & GIFTS:

THINGS TOO LARGE, FRAGILE OR EXPENSIVE TO BUY:

NOTEWORTHY SIGHTS OR EXPERIENCES:

MEMORABLE ENCOUNTERS:

TRAIN TICKETSPHOTOGRAPHSRECIEPTSBEVERAG
ECOASTERSMATCHBOOKSLEAVESBROCHURESPA
PER CURRENCYSUBWAY TICKETSMUSEUM PASSES
BUSINESS CARDSTOLLBOOTH RECIEPTSPRESSED F
LOWERSCANDY WRAPPERSMAPSWINE LABELSLU
GGAGE TAGSHOTEL STATIONARYFERRY TICKETSF
HONECARDSMOVIE & THEATER TICKETSMENUSPA
SSPORT PHOTOSPARKING TICKETSTRAIN TICKETS
PHOTOGRAPHSRECIEPTSBEVERAGECOASTERSM
ATCHBOOKSLEAVESBROCHURESPAPER CURRENC
YSUBWAY TICKETSMUSEUM PASSESBUSINESS CA
RDSTOLLBOOTH RECIEPTSPRESSED FLOWERSCAN
DY WRAPPERSMAPSWINE LABELSLUGGAGE TAGS
HOTEL STATIONARYFERRY TICKETSPHONECARDS
MOVIE & THEATER TICKETSMENUSPASSPORT PHO
TOSPARKING TICKETSTRAIN TICKETSPHOTOGRAP
HSRECIEPTSBEVERAGECOASTERSMATCHBOOKSL
EAVESBROCHURESPAPER CURRENCYSUBWAY TIC
KETSMUSEUM PASSESBUSINESS CARDSTOLLBOO
TH RECIEPTSPRESSED FLOWERSCANDY WRAPPER
SMAPSWINE LABELSLUGGAGE TAGSHOTEL STATI
ONARYFERRY TICKETSPHONECARDSMOVIE & THE
ATER TICKETSMENUSPASSPORT PHOTOSPARKING
TICKETSTRAIN TICKETSPHOTOGRAPHSRECIEPTSB
EVERAGECOASTERSMATCHBOOKSLEAVESBROC
HURESPAPER CURRENCYSUBWAY TICKETSMUSEU
M PASSESBUSINESS CARDSTOLLBOOTH RECIEPTS
PRESSED FLOWERSCANDY WRAPPERSMAPSWINE
LABELSLUGGAGE TAGSHOTEL STATIONARYFERRY
TICKETSPHONECARDSMOVIE & THEATER TICKETS
MENUSPASSPORT PHOTOSPARKING TICKETSTRAI
N TICKETSPHOTOGRAPHSRECIEPTSBEVERAGECO
ASTERSMATCHBOOKSLEAVESBROCHURESPAPER
CURRENCYSUBWAY TICKETSMUSEUM PASSESBUS
INESS CARDSTOLLBOOTH RECIEPTSPRESSED FLO
WERSCANDY WRAPPERSMAPSWINE LABELSLUG
GAGE TAGSHOTEL STATIONARYFERRY TICKETSPH
ONECARDSMOVIE & THEATER TICKETSMENUSPAS
SPORT PHOTOSPARKING TICKETSTRAIN TICKETSP

PASTE HERE

DATE:

DAY 13

LOCATION:

LODGING:

TRANSPORTATION:

PLACES VISITED:

MEALS, RESTAURANTS, SPECIAL DISHES:

TRAIN TICKETSPHOTOGRAPHSRECIEPTSBEVERAG
ECOASTERSMATCHBOOKSLEAVESBROCHURESPA
PER CURRENCYSUBWAY TICKETSMUSEUM PASSES
BUSINESS CARDSTOLLBOOTH RECIEPTSPRESSED F
LOWERSCANDY WRAPPERSMAPSWINE LABELSLU
GGAGE TAGSHOTEL STATIONARYFERRY TICKETSF
HONECARDSMOVIE & THEATER TICKETSMENUSPA
SSPORT PHOTOSPARKING TICKETSTRAIN TICKETS
PHOTOGRAPHSRECIEPTSBEVERAGECOASTERSM
ATCHBOOKSLEAVESBROCHURESPAPER CURRENC
YSUBWAY TICKETSMUSEUM PASSESBUSINESS CA
RDSTOLLBOOTH RECIEPTSPRESSED FLOWERSCAN
DY WRAPPERSMAPSWINE LABELSLUGGAGE TAGS
HOTEL STATIONARYFERRY TICKETSPHONECARDS
MOVIE & THEATER TICKETSMENUSPASSPORT PHO
TOSPARKING TICKETSTRAIN TICKETSPHOTOGRAP
HSRECIEPTSBEVERAGECOASTERSMATCHBOOKSL
EAVESBROCHURESPAPER CURRENCYSUBWAY TIC
KETSMUSEUM PASSESBUSINESS CARDSTOLLBOO
TH RECIEPTSPRESSED FLOWERSCANDY WRAPPER
SMAPSWINE LABELSLUGGAGE TAGSHOTEL STATI
ONARYFERRY TICKETSPHONECARDSMOVIE & THE
ATER TICKETSMENUSPASSPORT PHOTOSPARKING
TICKETSTRAIN TICKETSPHOTOGRAPHSRECIEPTSB
EVERAGECOASTERSMATCHBOOKSLEAVESBROC
HURESPAPER CURRENCYSUBWAY TICKETSMUSEU
M PASSESBUSINESS CARDSTOLLBOOTH RECIEPTS
PRESSED FLOWERSCANDY WRAPPERSMAPSWINE
LABELSLUGGAGE TAGSHOTEL STATIONARYFERRY
TICKETSPHONECARDSMOVIE & THEATER TICKETS
MENUSPASSPORT PHOTOSPARKING TICKETSTRAI
N TICKETSPHOTOGRAPHSRECIEPTSBEVERAGECO
ASTERSMATCHBOOKSLEAVESBROCHURESPAPER
CURRENCYSUBWAY TICKETSMUSEUM PASSESBUS
INESS CARDSTOLLBOOTH RECIEPTSPRESSED FLO
WERSCANDY WRAPPERSMAPSWINE LABELSLUG
GAGE TAGSHOTEL STATIONARYFERRY TICKETSPH
ONECARDSMOVIE & THEATER TICKETSMENUSPAS
SPORT PHOTOSPARKING TICKETSTRAIN TICKETSP

PASTE HERE

INTERESTING SHOPS:

ACQUISITIONS & GIFTS:

THINGS TOO LARGE, FRAGILE OR EXPENSIVE TO BUY:

NOTEWORTHY SIGHTS OR EXPERIENCES:

MEMORABLE ENCOUNTERS:

TRAIN TICKETSPHOTOGRAPHSRECIEPTSBEVERAG
ECOASTERSMATCHBOOKSLEAVESBROCHURESPA
PER CURRENCYSUBWAY TICKETSMUSEUM PASSES
BUSINESS CARDSTOLLBOOTH RECIEPTSPRESSED F
LOWERSCANDY WRAPPERSMAPSWINE LABELSLU
GGAGE TAGSHOTEL STATIONARYFERRY TICKETSP
HONECARDSMOVIE & THEATER TICKETSMENUSPA
SSPORT PHOTOSPARKING TICKETSTRAIN TICKETS
PHOTOGRAPHSRECIEPTSBEVERAGECOASTERSM
ATCHBOOKSLEAVESBROCHURESPAPER CURRENC
YSUBWAY TICKETSMUSEUM PASSESBUSINESS CA
RDSTOLLBOOTH RECIEPTSPRESSED FLOWERSCAN
DY WRAPPERSMAPSWINE LABELSLUGGAGE TAGS
HOTEL STATIONARYFERRY TICKETSPHONECARDS
MOVIE & THEATER TICKETSMENUSPASSPORT PHO
TOSPARKING TICKETSTRAIN TICKETSPHOTOGRAP
HSRECIEPTSBEVERAGECOASTERSMATCHBOOKSL
EAVESBROCHURESPAPER CURRENCYSUBWAY TIC
KETSMUSEUM PASSESBUSINESS CARDSTOLLBOO
TH RECIEPTSPRESSED FLOWERSCANDY WRAPPER
SMAPSWINE LABELSLUGGAGE TAGSHOTEL STATI
ONARYFERRY TICKETSPHONECARDSMOVIE & THE
ATER TICKETSMENUSPASSPORT PHOTOSPARKING
TICKETSTRAIN TICKETSPHOTOGRAPHSRECIEPTSB
EVERAGECOASTERSMATCHBOOKSLEAVESBROC
HURESPAPER CURRENCYSUBWAY TICKETSMUSEU
M PASSESBUSINESS CARDSTOLLBOOTH RECIEPTS
PRESSED FLOWERSCANDY WRAPPERSMAPSWINE
LABELSLUGGAGE TAGSHOTEL STATIONARYFERRY
TICKETSPHONECARDSMOVIE & THEATER TICKETS
MENUSPASSPORT PHOTOSPARKING TICKETSTRAI
N TICKETSPHOTOGRAPHSRECIEPTSBEVERAGECO
ASTERSMATCHBOOKSLEAVESBROCHURESPAPER
CURRENCYSUBWAY TICKETSMUSEUM PASSESBUS
INESS CARDSTOLLBOOTH RECIEPTSPRESSED FLO
WERSCANDY WRAPPERSMAPSWINE LABELSLUG
GAGE TAGSHOTEL STATIONARYFERRY TICKETSPH
ONECARDSMOVIE & THEATER TICKETSMENUSPAS
SPORT PHOTOSPARKING TICKETSTRAIN TICKETSP

PASTE HERE

DAY 14 DAY

DATE: _____

_____

LOCATION: _____

_____

LODGING: _____

_____

TRANSPORTATION: _____

_____

_____

PLACES VISITED: _____

_____

_____

_____

_____

_____

_____

_____

MEALS, RESTAURANTS, SPECIAL DISHES: _____

_____

_____

_____

_____

_____

_____

_____

TRAIN TICKETSPHOTOGRAPHSRECIEPTSBEVERAG
ECOASTERSMATCHBOOKSLEAVESBROCHURESPA
PER CURRENCYSUBWAY TICKETSMUSEUM PASSES
BUSINESS CARDSTOLLBOOTH RECIEPTSPRESSED F
LOWERSCANDY WRAPPERSMAPSWINE LABELSLU
GGAGE TAGSHOTEL STATIONARYFERRY TICKETSP
HONECARDSMOVIE & THEATER TICKETSMENUSPA
SSPORT PHOTOSPARKING TICKETSTRAIN TICKETS
PHOTOGRAPHSRECIEPTSBEVERAGECOASTERSM
ATCHBOOKSLEAVESBROCHURESPAPER CURRENC
YSUBWAY TICKETSMUSEUM PASSESBUSINESS CA
RDSTOLLBOOTH RECIEPTSPRESSED FLOWERSCAN
DY WRAPPERSMAPSWINE LABELSLUGGAGE TAGS
HOTEL STATIONARYFERRY TICKETSPHONECARDS
MOVIE & THEATER TICKETSMENUSPASSPORT PHO
TOSPARKING TICKETSTRAIN TICKETSPHOTOGRAP
HSRECIEPTSBEVERAGECOASTERSMATCHBOOKSL
EAVESBROCHURESPAPER CURRENCYSUBWAY TIC
KETSMUSEUM PASSESBUSINESS CARDSTOLLBOO
TH RECIEPTSPRESSED FLOWERSCANDY WRAPPER
SMAPSWINE LABELSLUGGAGE TAGSHOTEL STATI
ONARYFERRY TICKETSPHONECARDSMOVIE & THE
ATER TICKETSMENUSPASSPORT PHOTOSPARKING
TICKETSTRAIN TICKETSPHOTOGRAPHSRECIEPTSB
EVERAGECOASTERSMATCHBOOKSLEAVESBROC
HURESPAPER CURRENCYSUBWAY TICKETSMUSEU
M PASSESBUSINESS CARDSTOLLBOOTH RECIEPTS
PRESSED FLOWERSCANDY WRAPPERSMAPSWINE
LABELSLUGGAGE TAGSHOTEL STATIONARYFERRY
TICKETSPHONECARDSMOVIE & THEATER TICKETS
MENUSPASSPORT PHOTOSPARKING TICKETSTRAI
N TICKETSPHOTOGRAPHSRECIEPTSBEVERAGECO
ASTERSMATCHBOOKSLEAVESBROCHURESPAPER
CURRENCYSUBWAY TICKETSMUSEUM PASSESBUS
INESS CARDSTOLLBOOTH RECIEPTSPRESSED FLO
WERSCANDY WRAPPERSMAPSWINE LABELSLUG
GAGE TAGSHOTEL STATIONARYFERRY TICKETSPH
ONECARDSMOVIE & THEATER TICKETSMENUSPAS
SPORT PHOTOSPARKING TICKETSTRAIN TICKETSP

PASTE HERE

INTERESTING SHOPS:

ACQUISITIONS & GIFTS:

THINGS TOO LARGE, FRAGILE OR EXPENSIVE TO BUY:

NOTEWORTHY SIGHTS OR EXPERIENCES:

MEMORABLE ENCOUNTERS:

WEEK

TRAIN TICKETSPHOTOGRAPHSRECIEPTSBEVERAG
ECOASTERSMATCHBOOKSLEAVESBROCHURESPA
PER CURRENCYSUBWAY TICKETSMUSEUM PASSES
BUSINESS CARDSTOLLBOOTH RECIEPTSPRESSED F
LOWERSCANDY WRAPPERSMAPSWINE LABELSLU
GGAGE TAGSHOTEL STATIONARYFERRY TICKETSP
HONECARDSMOVIE & THEATER TICKETSMENUSPA
SSPORT PHOTOSPARKING TICKETSTRAIN TICKETS
PHOTOGRAPHSRECIEPTSBEVERAGECOASTERSM
ATCHBOOKSLEAVESBROCHURESPAPER CURRENC
YSUBWAY TICKETSMUSEUM PASSESBUSINESS CA
RDSTOLLBOOTH RECIEPTSPRESSED FLOWERSCAN
DY WRAPPERSMAPSWINE LABELSLUGGAGE TAGS
HOTEL STATIONARYFERRY TICKETSPHONECARDS
MOVIE & THEATER TICKETSMENUSPASSPORT PHO
TOSPARKING TICKETSTRAIN TICKETSPHOTOGRAP
HSRECIEPTSBEVERAGECOASTERSMATCHBOOKSL
EAVESBROCHURESPAPER CURRENCYSUBWAY TIC
KETSMUSEUM PASSESBUSINESS CARDSTOLLBOO
TH RECIEPTSPRESSED FLOWERSCANDY WRAPPER
SMAPSWINE LABELSLUGGAGE TAGSHOTEL STATI
ONARYFERRY TICKETSPHONECARDSMOVIE & THE
ATER TICKETSMENUSPASSPORT PHOTOSPARKING
TICKETSTRAIN TICKETSPHOTOGRAPHSRECIEPTSB
EVERAGECOASTERSMATCHBOOKSLEAVESBROC
HURESPAPER CURRENCYSUBWAY TICKETSMUSEU
M PASSESBUSINESS CARDSTOLLBOOTH RECIEPTS
PRESSED FLOWERSCANDY WRAPPERSMAPSWINE
LABELSLUGGAGE TAGSHOTEL STATIONARYFERRY
TICKETSPHONECARDSMOVIE & THEATER TICKETS
MENUSPASSPORT PHOTOSPARKING TICKETSTRAI
N TICKETSPHOTOGRAPHSRECIEPTSBEVERAGECO
ASTERSMATCHBOOKSLEAVESBROCHURESPAPER
CURRENCYSUBWAY TICKETSMUSEUM PASSESBUS
INESS CARDSTOLLBOOTH RECIEPTSPRESSED FLO
WERSCANDY WRAPPERSMAPSWINE LABELSLUG
GAGE TAGSHOTEL STATIONARYFERRY TICKETSPH
ONECARDSMOVIE & THEATER TICKETSMENUSPAS
SPORT PHOTOSPARKING TICKETSTRAIN TICKETSP

PASTE HERE

DATE:

LOCATION:

LODGING:

TRANSPORTATION:

PLACES VISITED:

MEALS, RESTAURANTS, SPECIAL DISHES:

TRAIN TICKETSPHOTOGRAPHSRECIEPTSBEVERAG
ECOASTERSMATCHBOOKSLEAVESBROCHURESPA
PER CURRENCYSUBWAY TICKETSMUSEUM PASSES
BUSINESS CARDSTOLLBOOTH RECIEPTSPRESSED F
LOWERSCANDY WRAPPERSMAPSWINE LABELSLU
GGAGE TAGSHOTEL STATIONARYFERRY TICKETSP
HONECARDSMOVIE & THEATER TICKETSMENUSPA
SSPORT PHOTOSPARKING TICKETSTRAIN TICKETS
PHOTOGRAPHSRECIEPTSBEVERAGECOASTERSM
ATCHBOOKSLEAVESBROCHURESPAPER CURRENC
YSUBWAY TICKETSMUSEUM PASSESBUSINESS CA
RDSTOLLBOOTH RECIEPTSPRESSED FLOWERSCAN
DY WRAPPERSMAPSWINE LABELSLUGGAGE TAGS
HOTEL STATIONARYFERRY TICKETSPHONECARDS
MOVIE & THEATER TICKETSMENUSPASSPORT PHO
TOSPARKING TICKETSTRAIN TICKETSPHOTOGRAP
HSRECIEPTSBEVERAGECOASTERSMATCHBOOKSL
EAVESBROCHURESPAPER CURRENCYSUBWAY TIC
KETSMUSEUM PASSESBUSINESS CARDSTOLLBOO
TH RECIEPTSPRESSED FLOWERSCANDY WRAPPER
SMAPSWINE LABELSLUGGAGE TAGSHOTEL STATI
ONARYFERRY TICKETSPHONECARDSMOVIE & THE
ATER TICKETSMENUSPASSPORT PHOTOSPARKING
TICKETSTRAIN TICKETSPHOTOGRAPHSRECIEPTSB
EVERAGECOASTERSMATCHBOOKSLEAVESBROC
HURESPAPER CURRENCYSUBWAY TICKETSMUSEU
M PASSESBUSINESS CARDSTOLLBOOTH RECIEPTS
PRESSED FLOWERSCANDY WRAPPERSMAPSWINE
LABELSLUGGAGE TAGSHOTEL STATIONARYFERRY
TICKETSPHONECARDSMOVIE & THEATER TICKETS
MENUSPASSPORT PHOTOSPARKING TICKETSTRAI
N TICKETSPHOTOGRAPHSRECIEPTSBEVERAGECO
ASTERSMATCHBOOKSLEAVESBROCHURESPAPER
CURRENCYSUBWAY TICKETSMUSEUM PASSESBUS
INESS CARDSTOLLBOOTH RECIEPTSPRESSED FLO
WERSCANDY WRAPPERSMAPSWINE LABELSLUG
GAGE TAGSHOTEL STATIONARYFERRY TICKETSPH
ONECARDSMOVIE & THEATER TICKETSMENUSPAS
SPORT PHOTOSPARKING TICKETSTRAIN TICKETSP

PASTE HERE

INTERESTING SHOPS:

ACQUISITIONS & GIFTS:

THINGS TOO LARGE, FRAGILE OR EXPENSIVE TO BUY:

NOTEWORTHY SIGHTS OR EXPERIENCES:

MEMORABLE ENCOUNTERS:

TRAIN TICKETSPHOTOGRAPHSRECIEPTSBEVERAG
ECOASTERSMATCHBOOKSLEAVESBROCHURESPA
PER CURRENCYSUBWAY TICKETSMUSEUM PASSES
BUSINESS CARDSTOLLBOOTH RECIEPTSPRESSED F
LOWERSCANDY WRAPPERSMAPSWINE LABELSLU
GGAGE TAGSHOTEL STATIONARYFERRY TICKETSP
HONECARDSMOVIE & THEATER TICKETSMENUSPA
SSPORT PHOTOSPARKING TICKETSTRAIN TICKETS
PHOTOGRAPHSRECIEPTSBEVERAGECOASTERSM
ATCHBOOKSLEAVESBROCHURESPAPER CURRENC
YSUBWAY TICKETSMUSEUM PASSESBUSINESS CA
RDSTOLLBOOTH RECIEPTSPRESSED FLOWERSCAN
DY WRAPPERSMAPSWINE LABELSLUGGAGE TAGS
HOTEL STATIONARYFERRY TICKETSPHONECARDS
MOVIE & THEATER TICKETSMENUSPASSPORT PHO
TOSPARKING TICKETSTRAIN TICKETSPHOTOGRAP
HSRECIEPTSBEVERAGECOASTERSMATCHBOOKSL
EAVESBROCHURESPAPER CURRENCYSUBWAY TIC
KETSMUSEUM PASSESBUSINESS CARDSTOLLBOO
TH RECIEPTSPRESSED FLOWERSCANDY WRAPPER
SMAPSWINE LABELSLUGGAGE TAGSHOTEL STATI
ONARYFERRY TICKETSPHONECARDSMOVIE & THE
ATER TICKETSMENUSPASSPORT PHOTOSPARKING
TICKETSTRAIN TICKETSPHOTOGRAPHSRECIEPTSB
EVERAGECOASTERSMATCHBOOKSLEAVESBROC
HURESPAPER CURRENCYSUBWAY TICKETSMUSEU
M PASSESBUSINESS CARDSTOLLBOOTH RECIEPTS
PRESSED FLOWERSCANDY WRAPPERSMAPSWINE
LABELSLUGGAGE TAGSHOTEL STATIONARYFERRY
TICKETSPHONECARDSMOVIE & THEATER TICKETS
MENUSPASSPORT PHOTOSPARKING TICKETSTRAI
N TICKETSPHOTOGRAPHSRECIEPTSBEVERAGECO
ASTERSMATCHBOOKSLEAVESBROCHURESPAPER
CURRENCYSUBWAY TICKETSMUSEUM PASSESBUS
INESS CARDSTOLLBOOTH RECIEPTSPRESSED FLO
WERSCANDY WRAPPERSMAPSWINE LABELSLUG
GAGE TAGSHOTEL STATIONARYFERRY TICKETSPH
ONECARDSMOVIE & THEATER TICKETSMENUSPAS
SPORT PHOTOSPARKING TICKETSTRAIN TICKETSP

PASTE HERE

SPLENDID HOTEL DE ROME

DATE:

LOCATION:

LODGING:

TRANSPORTATION:

PLACES VISITED:

MEALS, RESTAURANTS, SPECIAL DISHES:

TRAIN TICKETSPHOTOGRAPHSRECIEPTSBEVERAGECOASTERSMATCHBOOKSLEAVESBROCHURESPAPER CURRENCYSUBWAY TICKETSMUSEUM PASSESBUSINESS CARDSTOLLBOOTH RECIEPTSPRESSED FLOWERSCANDY WRAPPERSMAPSWINE LABELSLUGGAGE TAGSHOTEL STATIONARYFERRY TICKETSPHONECARDSMOVIE & THEATER TICKETSMENUSPASSPORT PHOTOSPARKING TICKETSTRAIN TICKETSPHOTOGRAPHSRECIEPTSBEVERAGECOASTERSMATCHBOOKSLEAVESBROCHURESPAPER CURRENCYSUBWAY TICKETSMUSEUM PASSESBUSINESS CARDSTOLLBOOTH RECIEPTSPRESSED FLOWERSCANDY WRAPPERSMAPSWINE LABELSLUGGAGE TAGSHOTEL STATIONARYFERRY TICKETSPHONECARDSMOVIE & THEATER TICKETSMENUSPASSPORT PHOTOSPARKING TICKETSTRAIN TICKETSPHOTOGRAPHSRECIEPTSBEVERAGECOASTERSMATCHBOOKSLEAVESBROCHURESPAPER CURRENCYSUBWAY TICKETSMUSEUM PASSESBUSINESS CARDSTOLLBOOTH RECIEPTSPRESSED FLOWERSCANDY WRAPPERSMAPSWINE LABELSLUGGAGE TAGSHOTEL STATIONARYFERRY TICKETSPHONECARDSMOVIE & THEATER TICKETSMENUSPASSPORT PHOTOSPARKING TICKETSTRAIN TICKETSPHOTOGRAPHSRECIEPTSBEVERAGECOASTERSMATCHBOOKSLEAVESBROCHURESPAPER CURRENCYSUBWAY TICKETSMUSEUM PASSESBUSINESS CARDSTOLLBOOTH RECIEPTSPRESSED FLOWERSCANDY WRAPPERSMAPSWINE LABELSLUGGAGE TAGSHOTEL STATIONARYFERRY TICKETSPHONECARDSMOVIE & THEATER TICKETSMENUSPASSPORT PHOTOSPARKING TICKETSTRAIN TICKETSPHOTOGRAPHSRECIEPTSBEVERAGECOASTERSMATCHBOOKSLEAVESBROCHURESPAPER CURRENCYSUBWAY TICKETSMUSEUM PASSESBUSINESS CARDSTOLLBOOTH RECIEPTSPRESSED FLOWERSCANDY WRAPPERSMAPSWINE LABELSLUGGAGE TAGSHOTEL STATIONARYFERRY TICKETSPHONECARDSMOVIE & THEATER TICKETSMENUSPASSPORT PHOTOSPARKING TICKETSTRAIN TICKETSP

PASTE HERE

INTERESTING SHOPS:

ACQUISITIONS & GIFTS:

THINGS TOO LARGE, FRAGILE OR EXPENSIVE TO BUY:

NOTEWORTHY SIGHTS OR EXPERIENCES:

MEMORABLE ENCOUNTERS:

TRAIN TICKETSPHOTOGRAPHSRECIEPTSBEVERAG
ECOASTERSMATCHBOOKSLEAVESBROCHURESPA
PER CURRENCYSUBWAY TICKETSMUSEUM PASSES
BUSINESS CARDSTOLLBOOTH RECIEPTSPRESSED F
LOWERSCANDY WRAPPERSMAPSWINE LABELSLU
GGAGE TAGSHOTEL STATIONARYFERRY TICKETSP
HONECARDSMOVIE & THEATER TICKETSMENUSPA
SSPORT PHOTOSPARKING TICKETSTRAIN TICKETS
PHOTOGRAPHSRECIEPTSBEVERAGECOASTERSM
ATCHBOOKSLEAVESBROCHURESPAPER CURRENC
YSUBWAY TICKETSMUSEUM PASSESBUSINESS CA
RDSTOLLBOOTH RECIEPTSPRESSED FLOWERSCAN
DY WRAPPERSMAPSWINE LABELSLUGGAGE TAGS
HOTEL STATIONARYFERRY TICKETSPHONECARDS
MOVIE & THEATER TICKETSMENUSPASSPORT PHO
TOSPARKING TICKETSTRAIN TICKETSPHOTOGRAP
HSRECIEPTSBEVERAGECOASTERSMATCHBOOKSL
EAVESBROCHURESPAPER CURRENCYSUBWAY TIC
KETSMUSEUM PASSESBUSINESS CARDSTOLLBOO
TH RECIEPTSPRESSED FLOWERSCANDY WRAPPER
SMAPSWINE LABELSLUGGAGE TAGSHOTEL STATI
ONARYFERRY TICKETSPHONECARDSMOVIE & THE
ATER TICKETSMENUSPASSPORT PHOTOSPARKING
TICKETSTRAIN TICKETSPHOTOGRAPHSRECIEPTSB
EVERAGECOASTERSMATCHBOOKSLEAVESBROC
HURESPAPER CURRENCYSUBWAY TICKETSMUSEU
M PASSESBUSINESS CARDSTOLLBOOTH RECIEPTS
PRESSED FLOWERSCANDY WRAPPERSMAPSWINE
LABELSLUGGAGE TAGSHOTEL STATIONARYFERRY
TICKETSPHONECARDSMOVIE & THEATER TICKETS
MENUSPASSPORT PHOTOSPARKING TICKETSTRAI
N TICKETSPHOTOGRAPHSRECIEPTSBEVERAGECO
ASTERSMATCHBOOKSLEAVESBROCHURESPAPER
CURRENCYSUBWAY TICKETSMUSEUM PASSESBUS
INESS CARDSTOLLBOOTH RECIEPTSPRESSED FLO
WERSCANDY WRAPPERSMAPSWINE LABELSLUG
GAGE TAGSHOTEL STATIONARYFERRY TICKETSPH
ONECARDSMOVIE & THEATER TICKETSMENUSPAS
SPORT PHOTOSPARKING TICKETSTRAIN TICKETSP

PASTE HERE

DATE:

LOCATION:

LODGING:

TRANSPORTATION:

PLACES VISITED:

MEALS, RESTAURANTS, SPECIAL DISHES:

TRAIN TICKETSPHOTOGRAPHSRECIEPTSBEVERAG
ECOASTERSMATCHBOOKSLEAVESBROCHURESPA
PER CURRENCYSUBWAY TICKETSMUSEUM PASSES
BUSINESS CARDSTOLLBOOTH RECIEPTSPRESSED F
LOWERSCANDY WRAPPERSMAPSWINE LABELSLU
GGAGE TAGSHOTEL STATIONARYFERRY TICKETSP
HONECARDSMOVIE & THEATER TICKETSMENUSPA
SSPORT PHOTOSPARKING TICKETSTRAIN TICKETS
PHOTOGRAPHSRECIEPTSBEVERAGECOASTERSM
ATCHBOOKSLEAVESBROCHURESPAPER CURRENC
YSUBWAY TICKETSMUSEUM PASSESBUSINESS CA
RDSTOLLBOOTH RECIEPTSPRESSED FLOWERSCAN
DY WRAPPERSMAPSWINE LABELSLUGGAGE TAGS
HOTEL STATIONARYFERRY TICKETSPHONECARDS
MOVIE & THEATER TICKETSMENUSPASSPORT PHO
TOSPARKING TICKETSTRAIN TICKETSPHOTOGRAP
HSRECIEPTSBEVERAGECOASTERSMATCHBOOKSL
EAVESBROCHURESPAPER CURRENCYSUBWAY TIC
KETSMUSEUM PASSESBUSINESS CARDSTOLLBOO
TH RECIEPTSPRESSED FLOWERSCANDY WRAPPER
SMAPSWINE LABELSLUGGAGE TAGSHOTEL STATI
ONARYFERRY TICKETSPHONECARDSMOVIE & THE
ATER TICKETSMENUSPASSPORT PHOTOSPARKING
TICKETSTRAIN TICKETSPHOTOGRAPHSRECIEPTSB
EVERAGECOASTERSMATCHBOOKSLEAVESBROC
HURESPAPER CURRENCYSUBWAY TICKETSMUSEU
M PASSESBUSINESS CARDSTOLLBOOTH RECIEPTS
PRESSED FLOWERSCANDY WRAPPERSMAPSWINE
LABELSLUGGAGE TAGSHOTEL STATIONARYFERRY
TICKETSPHONECARDSMOVIE & THEATER TICKETS
MENUSPASSPORT PHOTOSPARKING TICKETSTRAI
N TICKETSPHOTOGRAPHSRECIEPTSBEVERAGECO
ASTERSMATCHBOOKSLEAVESBROCHURESPAPER
CURRENCYSUBWAY TICKETSMUSEUM PASSESBUS
INESS CARDSTOLLBOOTH RECIEPTSPRESSED FLO
WERSCANDY WRAPPERSMAPSWINE LABELSLUG
GAGE TAGSHOTEL STATIONARYFERRY TICKETSPH
ONECARDSMOVIE & THEATER TICKETSMENUSPAS
SPORT PHOTOSPARKING TICKETSTRAIN TICKETSP

PASTE HERE

DAY 17 DAY

INTERESTING SHOPS:

ACQUISITIONS & GIFTS:

THINGS TOO LARGE, FRAGILE OR EXPENSIVE TO BUY:

NOTEWORTHY SIGHTS OR EXPERIENCES:

MEMORABLE ENCOUNTERS:

TRAIN TICKETSPHOTOGRAPHSRECIEPTSBEVERAG
ECOASTERSMATCHBOOKSLEAVESBROCHURESPA
PER CURRENCYSUBWAY TICKETSMUSEUM PASSES
BUSINESS CARDSTOLLBOOTH RECIEPTSPRESSED F
LOWERSCANDY WRAPPERSMAPSWINE LABELSLU
GGAGE TAGSHOTEL STATIONARYFERRY TICKETSP
HONECARDSMOVIE & THEATER TICKETSMENUSPA
SSPORT PHOTOSPARKING TICKETSTRAIN TICKETS
PHOTOGRAPHSRECIEPTSBEVERAGECOASTERSM
ATCHBOOKSLEAVESBROCHURESPAPER CURRENC
YSUBWAY TICKETSMUSEUM PASSESBUSINESS CA
RDSTOLLBOOTH RECIEPTSPRESSED FLOWERSCAN
DY WRAPPERSMAPSWINE LABELSLUGGAGE TAGS
HOTEL STATIONARYFERRY TICKETSPHONECARDS
MOVIE & THEATER TICKETSMENUSPASSPORT PHO
TOSPARKING TICKETSTRAIN TICKETSPHOTOGRAP
HSRECIEPTSBEVERAGECOASTERSMATCHBOOKSL
EAVESBROCHURESPAPER CURRENCYSUBWAY TIC
KETSMUSEUM PASSESBUSINESS CARDSTOLLBOO
TH RECIEPTSPRESSED FLOWERSCANDY WRAPPER
SMAPSWINE LABELSLUGGAGE TAGSHOTEL STATI
ONARYFERRY TICKETSPHONECARDSMOVIE & THE
ATER TICKETSMENUSPASSPORT PHOTOSPARKING
TICKETSTRAIN TICKETSPHOTOGRAPHSRECIEPTSB
EVERAGECOASTERSMATCHBOOKSLEAVESBROC
HURESPAPER CURRENCYSUBWAY TICKETSMUSEU
M PASSESBUSINESS CARDSTOLLBOOTH RECIEPTS
PRESSED FLOWERSCANDY WRAPPERSMAPSWINE
LABELSLUGGAGE TAGSHOTEL STATIONARYFERRY
TICKETSPHONECARDSMOVIE & THEATER TICKETS
MENUSPASSPORT PHOTOSPARKING TICKETSTRAI
N TICKETSPHOTOGRAPHSRECIEPTSBEVERAGECO
ASTERSMATCHBOOKSLEAVESBROCHURESPAPER
CURRENCYSUBWAY TICKETSMUSEUM PASSESBUS
INESS CARDSTOLLBOOTH RECIEPTSPRESSED FLO
WERSCANDY WRAPPERSMAPSWINE LABELSLUG
GAGE TAGSHOTEL STATIONARYFERRY TICKETSPH
ONECARDSMOVIE & THEATER TICKETSMENUSPAS
SPORT PHOTOSPARKING TICKETSTRAIN TICKETSP

PASTE HERE

DATE:

LOCATION:

LODGING:

TRANSPORTATION:

PLACES VISITED:

MEALS, RESTAURANTS, SPECIAL DISHES:

TRAIN TICKETSPHOTOGRAPHSRECIEPTSBEVERAG
ECOASTERSMATCHBOOKSLEAVESBROCHURESPA
PER CURRENCYSUBWAY TICKETSMUSEUM PASSES
BUSINESS CARDSTOLLBOOTH RECIEPTSPRESSED F
LOWERSCANDY WRAPPERSMAPSWINE LABELSLU
GGAGE TAGSHOTEL STATIONARYFERRY TICKETSP
HONECARDSMOVIE & THEATER TICKETSMENUSPA
SSPORT PHOTOSPARKING TICKETSTRAIN TICKETS
PHOTOGRAPHSRECIEPTSBEVERAGECOASTERSM
ATCHBOOKSLEAVESBROCHURESPAPER CURRENC
YSUBWAY TICKETSMUSEUM PASSESBUSINESS CA
RDSTOLLBOOTH RECIEPTSPRESSED FLOWERSCAN
DY WRAPPERSMAPSWINE LABELSLUGGAGE TAGS
HOTEL STATIONARYFERRY TICKETSPHONECARDS
MOVIE & THEATER TICKETSMENUSPASSPORT PHO
TOSPARKING TICKETSTRAIN TICKETSPHOTOGRAP
HSRECIEPTSBEVERAGECOASTERSMATCHBOOKSL
EAVESBROCHURESPAPER CURRENCYSUBWAY TIC
KETSMUSEUM PASSESBUSINESS CARDSTOLLBOO
TH RECIEPTSPRESSED FLOWERSCANDY WRAPPER
SMAPSWINE LABELSLUGGAGE TAGSHOTEL STATI
ONARYFERRY TICKETSPHONECARDSMOVIE & THE
ATER TICKETSMENUSPASSPORT PHOTOSPARKING
TICKETSTRAIN TICKETSPHOTOGRAPHSRECIEPTSB
EVERAGECOASTERSMATCHBOOKSLEAVESBROC
HURESPAPER CURRENCYSUBWAY TICKETSMUSEU
M PASSESBUSINESS CARDSTOLLBOOTH RECIEPTS
PRESSED FLOWERSCANDY WRAPPERSMAPSWINE
LABELSLUGGAGE TAGSHOTEL STATIONARYFERRY
TICKETSPHONECARDSMOVIE & THEATER TICKETS
MENUSPASSPORT PHOTOSPARKING TICKETSTRAI
N TICKETSPHOTOGRAPHSRECIEPTSBEVERAGECO
ASTERSMATCHBOOKSLEAVESBROCHURESPAPER
CURRENCYSUBWAY TICKETSMUSEUM PASSESBUS
INESS CARDSTOLLBOOTH RECIEPTSPRESSED FLO
WERSCANDY WRAPPERSMAPSWINE LABELSLUG
GAGE TAGSHOTEL STATIONARYFERRY TICKETSPH
ONECARDSMOVIE & THEATER TICKETSMENUSPAS
SPORT PHOTOSPARKING TICKETSTRAIN TICKETSP

PASTE HERE

INTERESTING SHOPS:

_____

_____

_____

_____

_____

ACQUISITIONS & GIFTS:

_____

_____

_____

_____

_____

THINGS TOO LARGE, FRAGILE OR EXPENSIVE TO BUY:

_____

_____

_____

_____

_____

NOTEWORTHY SIGHTS OR EXPERIENCES:

_____

_____

_____

_____

_____

MEMORABLE ENCOUNTERS:

_____

_____

_____

_____

_____

TRAIN TICKETSPHOTOGRAPHSRECIEPTSBEVERAG
ECOASTERSMATCHBOOKSLEAVESBROCHURESPA
PER CURRENCYSUBWAY TICKETSMUSEUM PASSES
BUSINESS CARDSTOLLBOOTH RECIEPTSPRESSED F
LOWERSCANDY WRAPPERSMAPSWINE LABELSLU
GGAGE TAGSHOTEL STATIONARYFERRY TICKETSP
HONECARDSMOVIE & THEATER TICKETSMENUSPA
SSPORT PHOTOSPARKING TICKETSTRAIN TICKETS
PHOTOGRAPHSRECIEPTSBEVERAGECOASTERSM
ATCHBOOKSLEAVESBROCHURESPAPER CURRENC
YSUBWAY TICKETSMUSEUM PASSESBUSINESS CA
RDSTOLLBOOTH RECIEPTSPRESSED FLOWERSCAN
DY WRAPPERSMAPSWINE LABELSLUGGAGE TAGS
HOTEL STATIONARYFERRY TICKETSPHONECARDS
MOVIE & THEATER TICKETSMENUSPASSPORT PHO
TOSPARKING TICKETSTRAIN TICKETSPHOTOGRAP
HSRECIEPTSBEVERAGECOASTERSMATCHBOOKSL
EAVESBROCHURESPAPER CURRENCYSUBWAY TIC
KETSMUSEUM PASSESBUSINESS CARDSTOLLBOO
TH RECIEPTSPRESSED FLOWERSCANDY WRAPPER
SMAPSWINE LABELSLUGGAGE TAGSHOTEL STATI
ONARYFERRY TICKETSPHONECARDSMOVIE & THE
ATER TICKETSMENUSPASSPORT PHOTOSPARKING
TICKETSTRAIN TICKETSPHOTOGRAPHSRECIEPTSB
EVERAGECOASTERSMATCHBOOKSLEAVESBROC
HURESPAPER CURRENCYSUBWAY TICKETSMUSEU
M PASSESBUSINESS CARDSTOLLBOOTH RECIEPTS
PRESSED FLOWERSCANDY WRAPPERSMAPSWINE
LABELSLUGGAGE TAGSHOTEL STATIONARYFERRY
TICKETSPHONECARDSMOVIE & THEATER TICKETS
MENUSPASSPORT PHOTOSPARKING TICKETSTRAI
N TICKETSPHOTOGRAPHSRECIEPTSBEVERAGECO
ASTERSMATCHBOOKSLEAVESBROCHURESPAPER
CURRENCYSUBWAY TICKETSMUSEUM PASSESBUS
INESS CARDSTOLLBOOTH RECIEPTSPRESSED FLO
WERSCANDY WRAPPERSMAPSWINE LABELSLUG
GAGE TAGSHOTEL STATIONARYFERRY TICKETSPH
ONECARDSMOVIE & THEATER TICKETSMENUSPAS
SPORT PHOTOSPARKING TICKETSTRAIN TICKETSP

PASTE HERE

DATE:

LOCATION:

LODGING:

TRANSPORTATION:

PLACES VISITED:

MEALS, RESTAURANTS, SPECIAL DISHES:

TRAIN TICKETSPHOTOGRAPHSRECIEPTSBEVERAG
ECOASTERSMATCHBOOKSLEAVESBROCHURESPA
PER CURRENCYSUBWAY TICKETSMUSEUM PASSES
BUSINESS CARDSTOLLBOOTH RECIEPTSPRESSED F
LOWERSCANDY WRAPPERSMAPSWINE LABELSLU
GGAGE TAGSHOTEL STATIONARYFERRY TICKETSP
HONECARDSMOVIE & THEATER TICKETSMENUSPA
SSPORT PHOTOSPARKING TICKETSTRAIN TICKETS
PHOTOGRAPHSRECIEPTSBEVERAGECOASTERSM
ATCHBOOKSLEAVESBROCHURESPAPER CURRENC
YSUBWAY TICKETSMUSEUM PASSESBUSINESS CA
RDSTOLLBOOTH RECIEPTSPRESSED FLOWERSCAN
DY WRAPPERSMAPSWINE LABELSLUGGAGE TAGS
HOTEL STATIONARYFERRY TICKETSPHONECARDS
MOVIE & THEATER TICKETSMENUSPASSPORT PHO
TOSPARKING TICKETSTRAIN TICKETSPHOTOGRAP
HSRECIEPTSBEVERAGECOASTERSMATCHBOOKSL
EAVESBROCHURESPAPER CURRENCYSUBWAY TIC
KETSMUSEUM PASSESBUSINESS CARDSTOLLBOO
TH RECIEPTSPRESSED FLOWERSCANDY WRAPPER
SMAPSWINE LABELSLUGGAGE TAGSHOTEL STATI
ONARYFERRY TICKETSPHONECARDSMOVIE & THE
ATER TICKETSMENUSPASSPORT PHOTOSPARKING
TICKETSTRAIN TICKETSPHOTOGRAPHSRECIEPTSB
EVERAGECOASTERSMATCHBOOKSLEAVESBROC
HURESPAPER CURRENCYSUBWAY TICKETSMUSEU
M PASSESBUSINESS CARDSTOLLBOOTH RECIEPTS
PRESSED FLOWERSCANDY WRAPPERSMAPSWINE
LABELSLUGGAGE TAGSHOTEL STATIONARYFERRY
TICKETSPHONECARDSMOVIE & THEATER TICKETS
MENUSPASSPORT PHOTOSPARKING TICKETSTRAI
N TICKETSPHOTOGRAPHSRECIEPTSBEVERAGECO
ASTERSMATCHBOOKSLEAVESBROCHURESPAPER
CURRENCYSUBWAY TICKETSMUSEUM PASSESBUS
INESS CARDSTOLLBOOTH RECIEPTSPRESSED FLO
WERSCANDY WRAPPERSMAPSWINE LABELSLUG
GAGE TAGSHOTEL STATIONARYFERRY TICKETSPH
ONECARDSMOVIE & THEATER TICKETSMENUSPAS
SPORT PHOTOSPARKING TICKETSTRAIN TICKETSP

PASTE HERE

INTERESTING SHOPS:

ACQUISITIONS & GIFTS:

THINGS TOO LARGE, FRAGILE OR EXPENSIVE TO BUY:

NOTEWORTHY SIGHTS OR EXPERIENCES:

MEMORABLE ENCOUNTERS:

TRAIN TICKETSPHOTOGRAPHSRECIEPTSBEVERAGECOASTERSMATCHBOOKSLEAVESBROCHURESPAPER CURRENCYSUBWAY TICKETSMUSEUM PASSESBUSINESS CARDSTOLLBOOTH RECIEPTSPRESSED FLOWERSCANDY WRAPPERSMAPSWINE LABELSLUGGAGE TAGSHOTEL STATIONARYFERRY TICKETSPHONECARDSMOVIE & THEATER TICKETSMENUSPASSPORT PHOTOSPARKING TICKETSTRAIN TICKETSPHOTOGRAPHSRECIEPTSBEVERAGECOASTERSMATCHBOOKSLEAVESBROCHURESPAPER CURRENCYSUBWAY TICKETSMUSEUM PASSESBUSINESS CARDSTOLLBOOTH RECIEPTSPRESSED FLOWERSCANDY WRAPPERSMAPSWINE LABELSLUGGAGE TAGSHOTEL STATIONARYFERRY TICKETSPHONECARDSMOVIE & THEATER TICKETSMENUSPASSPORT PHOTOSPARKING TICKETSTRAIN TICKETSPHOTOGRAPHSRECIEPTSBEVERAGECOASTERSMATCHBOOKSLEAVESBROCHURESPAPER CURRENCYSUBWAY TICKETSMUSEUM PASSESBUSINESS CARDSTOLLBOOTH RECIEPTSPRESSED FLOWERSCANDY WRAPPERSMAPSWINE LABELSLUGGAGE TAGSHOTEL STATIONARYFERRY TICKETSPHONECARDSMOVIE & THEATER TICKETSMENUSPASSPORT PHOTOSPARKING TICKETSTRAIN TICKETSPHOTOGRAPHSRECIEPTSBEVERAGECOASTERSMATCHBOOKSLEAVESBROCHURESPAPER CURRENCYSUBWAY TICKETSMUSEUM PASSESBUSINESS CARDSTOLLBOOTH RECIEPTSPRESSED FLOWERSCANDY WRAPPERSMAPSWINE LABELSLUGGAGE TAGSHOTEL STATIONARYFERRY TICKETSPHONECARDSMOVIE & THEATER TICKETSMENUSPASSPORT PHOTOSPARKING TICKETSTRAIN TICKETSPHOTOGRAPHSRECIEPTSBEVERAGECOASTERSMATCHBOOKSLEAVESBROCHURESPAPER CURRENCYSUBWAY TICKETSMUSEUM PASSESBUSINESS CARDSTOLLBOOTH RECIEPTSPRESSED FLOWERSCANDY WRAPPERSMAPSWINE LABELSLUGGAGE TAGSHOTEL STATIONARYFERRY TICKETSPHONECARDSMOVIE & THEATER TICKETSMENUSPASSPORT PHOTOSPARKING TICKETSTRAIN TICKETSP

PASTE HERE

DATE:

LOCATION:

LODGING:

TRANSPORTATION:

PLACES VISITED:

MEALS, RESTAURANTS, SPECIAL DISHES:

TRAIN TICKETSPHOTOGRAPHSRECIEPTSBEVERAG
ECOASTERSMATCHBOOKSLEAVESBROCHURESPA
PER CURRENCYSUBWAY TICKETSMUSEUM PASSES
BUSINESS CARDSTOLLBOOTH RECIEPTSPRESSED F
LOWERSCANDY WRAPPERSMAPSWINE LABELSLU
GGAGE TAGSHOTEL STATIONARYFERRY TICKETSP
HONECARDSMOVIE & THEATER TICKETSMENUSPA
SSPORT PHOTOSPARKING TICKETSTRAIN TICKETS
PHOTOGRAPHSRECIEPTSBEVERAGECOASTERSM
ATCHBOOKSLEAVESBROCHURESPAPER CURRENC
YSUBWAY TICKETSMUSEUM PASSESBUSINESS CA
RDSTOLLBOOTH RECIEPTSPRESSED FLOWERSCAN
DY WRAPPERSMAPSWINE LABELSLUGGAGE TAGS
HOTEL STATIONARYFERRY TICKETSPHONECARDS
MOVIE & THEATER TICKETSMENUSPASSPORT PHO
TOSPARKING TICKETSTRAIN TICKETSPHOTOGRAP
HSRECIEPTSBEVERAGECOASTERSMATCHBOOKSL
EAVESBROCHURESPAPER CURRENCYSUBWAY TIC
KETSMUSEUM PASSESBUSINESS CARDSTOLLBOO
TH RECIEPTSPRESSED FLOWERSCANDY WRAPPER
SMAPSWINE LABELSLUGGAGE TAGSHOTEL STATI
ONARYFERRY TICKETSPHONECARDSMOVIE & THE
ATER TICKETSMENUSPASSPORT PHOTOSPARKING
TICKETSTRAIN TICKETSPHOTOGRAPHSRECIEPTSB
EVERAGECOASTERSMATCHBOOKSLEAVESBROC
HURESPAPER CURRENCYSUBWAY TICKETSMUSEU
M PASSESBUSINESS CARDSTOLLBOOTH RECIEPTS
PRESSED FLOWERSCANDY WRAPPERSMAPSWINE
LABELSLUGGAGE TAGSHOTEL STATIONARYFERRY
TICKETSPHONECARDSMOVIE & THEATER TICKETS
MENUSPASSPORT PHOTOSPARKING TICKETSTRAI
N TICKETSPHOTOGRAPHSRECIEPTSBEVERAGECO
ASTERSMATCHBOOKSLEAVESBROCHURESPAPER
CURRENCYSUBWAY TICKETSMUSEUM PASSESBUS
INESS CARDSTOLLBOOTH RECIEPTSPRESSED FLO
WERSCANDY WRAPPERSMAPSWINE LABELSLUG
GAGE TAGSHOTEL STATIONARYFERRY TICKETSPH
ONECARDSMOVIE & THEATER TICKETSMENUSPAS
SPORT PHOTOSPARKING TICKETSTRAIN TICKETSP

PASTE HERE

DAY 20

INTERESTING SHOPS:

ACQUISITIONS & GIFTS:

THINGS TOO LARGE, FRAGILE OR EXPENSIVE TO BUY:

NOTEWORTHY SIGHTS OR EXPERIENCES:

MEMORABLE ENCOUNTERS:

TRAIN TICKETS PHOTOGRAPHS RECIEPTS BEVERAGE COASTERS MATCHBOOKS LEAVES BROCHURES PAPER CURRENCY SUBWAY TICKETS MUSEUM PASSES BUSINESS CARDS TOLLBOOTH RECIEPTS PRESSED FLOWERS CANDY WRAPPERS MAPS WINE LABELS LUGGAGE TAGS HOTEL STATIONARY FERRY TICKETS PHONE CARDS MOVIE & THEATER TICKETS MENUS PASSPORT PHOTOS PARKING TICKETS TRAIN TICKETS PHOTOGRAPHS RECIEPTS BEVERAGE COASTERS MATCHBOOKS LEAVES BROCHURES PAPER CURRENCY SUBWAY TICKETS MUSEUM PASSES BUSINESS CARDS TOLLBOOTH RECIEPTS PRESSED FLOWERS CANDY WRAPPERS MAPS WINE LABELS LUGGAGE TAGS HOTEL STATIONARY FERRY TICKETS PHONE CARDS MOVIE & THEATER TICKETS MENUS PASSPORT PHOTOS PARKING TICKETS TRAIN TICKETS PHOTOGRAPHS RECIEPTS BEVERAGE COASTERS MATCHBOOKS LEAVES BROCHURES PAPER CURRENCY SUBWAY TICKETS MUSEUM PASSES BUSINESS CARDS TOLLBOOTH RECIEPTS PRESSED FLOWERS CANDY WRAPPERS MAPS WINE LABELS LUGGAGE TAGS HOTEL STATIONARY FERRY TICKETS PHONE CARDS MOVIE & THEATER TICKETS MENUS PASSPORT PHOTOS PARKING TICKETS TRAIN TICKETS PHOTOGRAPHS RECIEPTS BEVERAGE COASTERS MATCHBOOKS LEAVES BROCHURES PAPER CURRENCY SUBWAY TICKETS MUSEUM PASSES BUSINESS CARDS TOLLBOOTH RECIEPTS PRESSED FLOWERS CANDY WRAPPERS MAPS WINE LABELS LUGGAGE TAGS HOTEL STATIONARY FERRY TICKETS PHONE CARDS MOVIE & THEATER TICKETS MENUS PASSPORT PHOTOS PARKING TICKETS TRAIN TICKETS PHOTOGRAPHS RECIEPTS BEVERAGE COASTERS MATCHBOOKS LEAVES BROCHURES PAPER CURRENCY SUBWAY TICKETS MUSEUM PASSES BUSINESS CARDS TOLLBOOTH RECIEPTS PRESSED FLOWERS CANDY WRAPPERS MAPS WINE LABELS LUGGAGE TAGS HOTEL STATIONARY FERRY TICKETS PHONE CARDS MOVIE & THEATER TICKETS MENUS PASSPORT PHOTOS PARKING TICKETS TRAIN TICKETS P

PASTE HERE

DATE:

LOCATION:

LODGING:

TRANSPORTATION:

PLACES VISITED:

MEALS, RESTAURANTS, SPECIAL DISHES:

TRAIN TICKETSPHOTOGRAPHSRECIEPTSBEVERAG
ECOASTERSMATCHBOOKSLEAVESBROCHURESPA
PER CURRENCYSUBWAY TICKETSMUSEUM PASSES
BUSINESS CARDSTOLLBOOTH RECIEPTSPRESSED F
LOWERSCANDY WRAPPERSMAPSWINE LABELSLU
GGAGE TAGSHOTEL STATIONARYFERRY TICKETSP
HONECARDSMOVIE & THEATER TICKETSMENUSPA
SSPORT PHOTOSPARKING TICKETSTRAIN TICKETS
PHOTOGRAPHSRECIEPTSBEVERAGECOASTERSM
ATCHBOOKSLEAVESBROCHURESPAPER CURRENC
YSUBWAY TICKETSMUSEUM PASSESBUSINESS CA
RDSTOLLBOOTH RECIEPTSPRESSED FLOWERSCAN
DY WRAPPERSMAPSWINE LABELSLUGGAGE TAGS
HOTEL STATIONARYFERRY TICKETSPHONECARDS
MOVIE & THEATER TICKETSMENUSPASSPORT PHO
TOSPARKING TICKETSTRAIN TICKETSPHOTOGRAP
HSRECIEPTSBEVERAGECOASTERSMATCHBOOKSL
EAVESBROCHURESPAPER CURRENCYSUBWAY TIC
KETSMUSEUM PASSESBUSINESS CARDSTOLLBOO
TH RECIEPTSPRESSED FLOWERSCANDY WRAPPER
SMAPSWINE LABELSLUGGAGE TAGSHOTEL STATI
ONARYFERRY TICKETSPHONECARDSMOVIE & THE
ATER TICKETSMENUSPASSPORT PHOTOSPARKING
TICKETSTRAIN TICKETSPHOTOGRAPHSRECIEPTSB
EVERAGECOASTERSMATCHBOOKSLEAVESBROC
HURESPAPER CURRENCYSUBWAY TICKETSMUSEU
M PASSESBUSINESS CARDSTOLLBOOTH RECIEPTS
PRESSED FLOWERSCANDY WRAPPERSMAPSWINE
LABELSLUGGAGE TAGSHOTEL STATIONARYFERRY
TICKETSPHONECARDSMOVIE & THEATER TICKETS
MENUSPASSPORT PHOTOSPARKING TICKETSTRAI
N TICKETSPHOTOGRAPHSRECIEPTSBEVERAGECO
ASTERSMATCHBOOKSLEAVESBROCHURESPAPER
CURRENCYSUBWAY TICKETSMUSEUM PASSESBUS
NESS CARDSTOLLBOOTH RECIEPTSPRESSED FLO
WERSCANDY WRAPPERSMAPSWINE LABELSLUG
GAGE TAGSHOTEL STATIONARYFERRY TICKETSPH
ONECARDSMOVIE & THEATER TICKETSMENUSPAS
SPORT PHOTOSPARKING TICKETSTRAIN TICKETSP

PASTE HERE

INTERESTING SHOPS:

ACQUISITIONS & GIFTS:

THINGS TOO LARGE, FRAGILE OR EXPENSIVE TO BUY:

NOTEWORTHY SIGHTS OR EXPERIENCES:

MEMORABLE ENCOUNTERS:

WEEK

4

TRAIN TICKETSPHOTOGRAPHSRECIEPTSBEVERAG
ECOASTERSMATCHBOOKSLEAVESBROCHURESPA
PER CURRENCYSUBWAY TICKETSMUSEUM PASSES
BUSINESS CARDSTOLLBOOTH RECIEPTSPRESSED F
LOWERSCANDY WRAPPERSMAPSWINE LABELSLU
GGAGE TAGSHOTEL STATIONARYFERRY TICKETSP
HONECARDSMOVIE & THEATER TICKETSMENUSPA
SSPORT PHOTOSPARKING TICKETSTRAIN TICKETS
PHOTOGRAPHSRECIEPTSBEVERAGECOASTERSM
ATCHBOOKSLEAVESBROCHURESPAPER CURRENC
YSUBWAY TICKETSMUSEUM PASSESBUSINESS CA
RDSTOLLBOOTH RECIEPTSPRESSED FLOWERSCAN
DY WRAPPERSMAPSWINE LABELSLUGGAGE TAGS
HOTEL STATIONARYFERRY TICKETSPHONECARDS
MOVIE & THEATER TICKETSMENUSPASSPORT PHO
TOSPARKING TICKETSTRAIN TICKETSPHOTOGRAP
HSRECIEPTSBEVERAGECOASTERSMATCHBOOKSL
EAVESBROCHURESPAPER CURRENCYSUBWAY TIC
KETSMUSEUM PASSESBUSINESS CARDSTOLLBOO
TH RECIEPTSPRESSED FLOWERSCANDY WRAPPER
SMAPSWINE LABELSLUGGAGE TAGSHOTEL STATI
ONARYFERRY TICKETSPHONECARDSMOVIE & THE
ATER TICKETSMENUSPASSPORT PHOTOSPARKING
TICKETSTRAIN TICKETSPHOTOGRAPHSRECIEPTSB
EVERAGECOASTERSMATCHBOOKSLEAVESBROC
HURESPAPER CURRENCYSUBWAY TICKETSMUSEU
M PASSESBUSINESS CARDSTOLLBOOTH RECIEPTS
PRESSED FLOWERSCANDY WRAPPERSMAPSWINE
LABELSLUGGAGE TAGSHOTEL STATIONARYFERRY
TICKETSPHONECARDSMOVIE & THEATER TICKETS
MENUSPASSPORT PHOTOSPARKING TICKETSTRAI
N TICKETSPHOTOGRAPHSRECIEPTSBEVERAGECO
ASTERSMATCHBOOKSLEAVESBROCHURESPAPER
CURRENCYSUBWAY TICKETSMUSEUM PASSESBUS
INESS CARDSTOLLBOOTH RECIEPTSPRESSED FLO
WERSCANDY WRAPPERSMAPSWINE LABELSLUG
GAGE TAGSHOTEL STATIONARYFERRY TICKETSPH
ONECARDSMOVIE & THEATER TICKETSMENUSPAS
SPORT PHOTOSPARKING TICKETSTRAIN TICKETSP

PASTEHERE

DATE: _____

_____

LOCATION:
_____
_____

LODGING:
_____
_____

TRANSPORTATION:
_____
_____
_____

PLACES VISITED:
_____
_____
_____
_____
_____
_____
_____
_____

MEALS, RESTAURANTS, SPECIAL DISHES:
_____
_____
_____
_____
_____
_____
_____
_____

TRAIN TICKETSPHOTOGRAPHSRECIEPTSBEVERAG
ECOASTERSMATCHBOOKSLEAVESBROCHURESPA
PER CURRENCYSUBWAY TICKETSMUSEUM PASSES
BUSINESS CARDSTOLLBOOTH RECIEPTSPRESSED F
LOWERSCANDY WRAPPERSMAPSWINE LABELSLU
GGAGE TAGSHOTEL STATIONARYFERRY TICKETSP
HONECARDSMOVIE & THEATER TICKETSMENUSPA
SSPORT PHOTOSPARKING TICKETSTRAIN TICKETS
PHOTOGRAPHSRECIEPTSBEVERAGECOASTERSM
ATCHBOOKSLEAVESBROCHURESPAPER CURRENC
YSUBWAY TICKETSMUSEUM PASSESBUSINESS CA
RDSTOLLBOOTH RECIEPTSPRESSED FLOWERSCAN
DY WRAPPERSMAPSWINE LABELSLUGGAGE TAGS
HOTEL STATIONARYFERRY TICKETSPHONECARDS
MOVIE & THEATER TICKETSMENUSPASSPORT PHO
TOSPARKING TICKETSTRAIN TICKETSPHOTOGRAP
HSRECIEPTSBEVERAGECOASTERSMATCHBOOKSL
EAVESBROCHURESPAPER CURRENCYSUBWAY TIC
KETSMUSEUM PASSESBUSINESS CARDSTOLLBOO
TH RECIEPTSPRESSED FLOWERSCANDY WRAPPER
SMAPSWINE LABELSLUGGAGE TAGSHOTEL STATI
ONARYFERRY TICKETSPHONECARDSMOVIE & THE
ATER TICKETSMENUSPASSPORT PHOTOSPARKING
TICKETSTRAIN TICKETSPHOTOGRAPHSRECIEPTSB
EVERAGECOASTERSMATCHBOOKSLEAVESBROC
HURESPAPER CURRENCYSUBWAY TICKETSMUSEU
M PASSESBUSINESS CARDSTOLLBOOTH RECIEPTS
PRESSED FLOWERSCANDY WRAPPERSMAPSWINE
LABELSLUGGAGE TAGSHOTEL STATIONARYFERRY
TICKETSPHONECARDSMOVIE & THEATER TICKETS
MENUSPASSPORT PHOTOSPARKING TICKETSTRAI
N TICKETSPHOTOGRAPHSRECIEPTSBEVERAGECO
ASTERSMATCHBOOKSLEAVESBROCHURESPAPER
CURRENCYSUBWAY TICKETSMUSEUM PASSESBUS
INESS CARDSTOLLBOOTH RECIEPTSPRESSED FLO
WERSCANDY WRAPPERSMAPSWINE LABELSLUG
GAGE TAGSHOTEL STATIONARYFERRY TICKETSPH
ONECARDSMOVIE & THEATER TICKETSMENUSPAS
SPORT PHOTOSPARKING TICKETSTRAIN TICKETSP

PASTE HERE

INTERESTING SHOPS:

ACQUISITIONS & GIFTS:

THINGS TOO LARGE, FRAGILE OR EXPENSIVE TO BUY:

NOTEWORTHY SIGHTS OR EXPERIENCES:

MEMORABLE ENCOUNTERS:

TRAIN TICKETSPHOTOGRAPHSRECIEPTSBEVERAG
ECOASTERSMATCHBOOKSLEAVESBROCHURESPA
PER CURRENCYSUBWAY TICKETSMUSEUM PASSES
BUSINESS CARDSTOLLBOOTH RECIEPTSPRESSED F
LOWERSCANDY WRAPPERSMAPSWINE LABELSLU
GGAGE TAGSHOTEL STATIONARYFERRY TICKETSP
HONECARDSMOVIE & THEATER TICKETSMENUSPA
SSPORT PHOTOSPARKING TICKETSTRAIN TICKETS
PHOTOGRAPHSRECIEPTSBEVERAGECOASTERSM
ATCHBOOKSLEAVESBROCHURESPAPER CURRENC
YSUBWAY TICKETSMUSEUM PASSESBUSINESS CA
RDSTOLLBOOTH RECIEPTSPRESSED FLOWERSCAN
DY WRAPPERSMAPSWINE LABELSLUGGAGE TAGS
HOTEL STATIONARYFERRY TICKETSPHONECARDS
MOVIE & THEATER TICKETSMENUSPASSPORT PHO
TOSPARKING TICKETSTRAIN TICKETSPHOTOGRAP
HSRECIEPTSBEVERAGECOASTERSMATCHBOOKSL
EAVESBROCHURESPAPER CURRENCYSUBWAY TIC
KETSMUSEUM PASSESBUSINESS CARDSTOLLBOO
TH RECIEPTSPRESSED FLOWERSCANDY WRAPPER
SMAPSWINE LABELSLUGGAGE TAGSHOTEL STATI
ONARYFERRY TICKETSPHONECARDSMOVIE & THE
ATER TICKETSMENUSPASSPORT PHOTOSPARKING
TICKETSTRAIN TICKETSPHOTOGRAPHSRECIEPTSB
EVERAGECOASTERSMATCHBOOKSLEAVESBROC
HURESPAPER CURRENCYSUBWAY TICKETSMUSEU
M PASSESBUSINESS CARDSTOLLBOOTH RECIEPTS
PRESSED FLOWERSCANDY WRAPPERSMAPSWINE
LABELSLUGGAGE TAGSHOTEL STATIONARYFERRY
TICKETSPHONECARDSMOVIE & THEATER TICKETS
MENUSPASSPORT PHOTOSPARKING TICKETSTRAI
N TICKETSPHOTOGRAPHSRECIEPTSBEVERAGECO
ASTERSMATCHBOOKSLEAVESBROCHURESPAPER
CURRENCYSUBWAY TICKETSMUSEUM PASSESBUS
INESS CARDSTOLLBOOTH RECIEPTSPRESSED FLO
WERSCANDY WRAPPERSMAPSWINE LABELSLUG
GAGE TAGSHOTEL STATIONARYFERRY TICKETSPH
ONECARDSMOVIE & THEATER TICKETSMENUSPAS
SPORT PHOTOSPARKING TICKETSTRAIN TICKETSP

PASTE HERE

DATE:

LOCATION:

LODGING:

TRANSPORTATION:

PLACES VISITED:

MEALS, RESTAURANTS, SPECIAL DISHES:

TRAIN TICKETSPHOTOGRAPHSRECIEPTSBEVERAG
ECOASTERSMATCHBOOKSLEAVESBROCHURESPA
PER CURRENCYSUBWAY TICKETSMUSEUM PASSES
BUSINESS CARDSTOLLBOOTH RECIEPTSPRESSED F
LOWERSCANDY WRAPPERSMAPSWINE LABELSLU
GGAGE TAGSHOTEL STATIONARYFERRY TICKETSP
HONECARDSMOVIE & THEATER TICKETSMENUSPA
SSPORT PHOTOSPARKING TICKETSTRAIN TICKETS
PHOTOGRAPHSRECIEPTSBEVERAGECOASTERSM
ATCHBOOKSLEAVESBROCHURESPAPER CURRENC
YSUBWAY TICKETSMUSEUM PASSESBUSINESS CA
RDSTOLLBOOTH RECIEPTSPRESSED FLOWERSCAN
DY WRAPPERSMAPSWINE LABELSLUGGAGE TAGS
HOTEL STATIONARYFERRY TICKETSPHONECARDS
MOVIE & THEATER TICKETSMENUSPASSPORT PHO
TOSPARKING TICKETSTRAIN TICKETSPHOTOGRAP
HSRECIEPTSBEVERAGECOASTERSMATCHBOOKSL
EAVESBROCHURESPAPER CURRENCYSUBWAY TIC
KETSMUSEUM PASSESBUSINESS CARDSTOLLBOO
TH RECIEPTSPRESSED FLOWERSCANDY WRAPPER
SMAPSWINE LABELSLUGGAGE TAGSHOTEL STATI
ONARYFERRY TICKETSPHONECARDSMOVIE & THE
ATER TICKETSMENUSPASSPORT PHOTOSPARKING
TICKETSTRAIN TICKETSPHOTOGRAPHSRECIEPTSB
EVERAGECOASTERSMATCHBOOKSLEAVESBROC
HURESPAPER CURRENCYSUBWAY TICKETSMUSEU
M PASSESBUSINESS CARDSTOLLBOOTH RECIEPTS
PRESSED FLOWERSCANDY WRAPPERSMAPSWINE
LABELSLUGGAGE TAGSHOTEL STATIONARYFERRY
TICKETSPHONECARDSMOVIE & THEATER TICKETS
MENUSPASSPORT PHOTOSPARKING TICKETSTRAI
N TICKETSPHOTOGRAPHSRECIEPTSBEVERAGECO
ASTERSMATCHBOOKSLEAVESBROCHURESPAPER
CURRENCYSUBWAY TICKETSMUSEUM PASSESBUS
INESS CARDSTOLLBOOTH RECIEPTSPRESSED FLO
WERSCANDY WRAPPERSMAPSWINE LABELSLUG
GAGE TAGSHOTEL STATIONARYFERRY TICKETSPH
ONECARDSMOVIE & THEATER TICKETSMENUSPAS
SPORT PHOTOSPARKING TICKETSTRAIN TICKETSP

PASTE HERE

INTERESTING SHOPS:

_____

_____

_____

_____

_____

_____

ACQUISITIONS & GIFTS:

_____

_____

_____

_____

_____

THINGS TOO LARGE, FRAGILE OR EXPENSIVE TO BUY:

_____

_____

_____

_____

NOTEWORTHY SIGHTS OR EXPERIENCES:

_____

_____

_____

_____

_____

MEMORABLE ENCOUNTERS:

_____

_____

_____

_____

_____

TRAIN TICKETSPHOTOGRAPHSRECIEPTSBEVERAG
ECOASTERSMATCHBOOKSLEAVESBROCHURESPA
PER CURRENCYSUBWAY TICKETSMUSEUM PASSES
BUSINESS CARDSTOLLBOOTH RECIEPTSPRESSED F
LOWERSCANDY WRAPPERSMAPSWINE LABELSLU
GGAGE TAGSHOTEL STATIONARYFERRY TICKETSP
HONECARDSMOVIE & THEATER TICKETSMENUSPA
SSPORT PHOTOSPARKING TICKETSTRAIN TICKETS
PHOTOGRAPHSRECIEPTSBEVERAGECOASTERSM
ATCHBOOKSLEAVESBROCHURESPAPER CURRENC
YSUBWAY TICKETSMUSEUM PASSESBUSINESS CA
RDSTOLLBOOTH RECIEPTSPRESSED FLOWERSCAN
DY WRAPPERSMAPSWINE LABELSLUGGAGE TAGS
HOTEL STATIONARYFERRY TICKETSPHONECARDS
MOVIE & THEATER TICKETSMENUSPASSPORT PHO
TOSPARKING TICKETSTRAIN TICKETSPHOTOGRAP
HSRECIEPTSBEVERAGECOASTERSMATCHBOOKSL
EAVESBROCHURESPAPER CURRENCYSUBWAY TIC
KETSMUSEUM PASSESBUSINESS CARDSTOLLBOO
TH RECIEPTSPRESSED FLOWERSCANDY WRAPPER
SMAPSWINE LABELSLUGGAGE TAGSHOTEL STATI
ONARYFERRY TICKETSPHONECARDSMOVIE & THE
ATER TICKETSMENUSPASSPORT PHOTOSPARKING
TICKETSTRAIN TICKETSPHOTOGRAPHSRECIEPTSB
EVERAGECOASTERSMATCHBOOKSLEAVESBROC
HURESPAPER CURRENCYSUBWAY TICKETSMUSEU
M PASSESBUSINESS CARDSTOLLBOOTH RECIEPTS
PRESSED FLOWERSCANDY WRAPPERSMAPSWINE
LABELSLUGGAGE TAGSHOTEL STATIONARYFERRY
TICKETSPHONECARDSMOVIE & THEATER TICKETS
MENUSPASSPORT PHOTOSPARKING TICKETSTRAI
N TICKETSPHOTOGRAPHSRECIEPTSBEVERAGECO
ASTERSMATCHBOOKSLEAVESBROCHURESPAPER
CURRENCYSUBWAY TICKETSMUSEUM PASSESBUS
INESS CARDSTOLLBOOTH RECIEPTSPRESSED FLO
WERSCANDY WRAPPERSMAPSWINE LABELSLUG
GAGE TAGSHOTEL STATIONARYFERRY TICKETSPH
ONECARDSMOVIE & THEATER TICKETSMENUSPAS
SPORT PHOTOSPARKING TICKETSTRAIN TICKETSP

PASTE HERE

DATE:

LOCATION:

LODGING:

TRANSPORTATION:

PLACES VISITED:

MEALS, RESTAURANTS, SPECIAL DISHES:

TRAIN TICKETSPHOTOGRAPHSRECIEPTSBEVERAG
ECOASTERSMATCHBOOKSLEAVESBROCHURESPA
PER CURRENCYSUBWAY TICKETSMUSEUM PASSES
BUSINESS CARDSTOLLBOOTH RECIEPTSPRESSED F
LOWERSCANDY WRAPPERSMAPSWINE LABELSLU
GGAGE TAGSHOTEL STATIONARYFERRY TICKETSP
HONECARDSMOVIE & THEATER TICKETSMENUSPA
SSPORT PHOTOSPARKING TICKETSTRAIN TICKETS
PHOTOGRAPHSRECIEPTSBEVERAGECOASTERSM
ATCHBOOKSLEAVESBROCHURESPAPER CURRENC
YSUBWAY TICKETSMUSEUM PASSESBUSINESS CA
RDSTOLLBOOTH RECIEPTSPRESSED FLOWERSCAN
DY WRAPPERSMAPSWINE LABELSLUGGAGE TAGS
HOTEL STATIONARYFERRY TICKETSPHONECARDS
MOVIE & THEATER TICKETSMENUSPASSPORT PHO
TOSPARKING TICKETSTRAIN TICKETSPHOTOGRAP
HSRECIEPTSBEVERAGECOASTERSMATCHBOOKSL
EAVESBROCHURESPAPER CURRENCYSUBWAY TIC
KETSMUSEUM PASSESBUSINESS CARDSTOLLBOO
TH RECIEPTSPRESSED FLOWERSCANDY WRAPPER
SMAPSWINE LABELSLUGGAGE TAGSHOTEL STATI
ONARYFERRY TICKETSPHONECARDSMOVIE & THE
ATER TICKETSMENUSPASSPORT PHOTOSPARKING
TICKETSTRAIN TICKETSPHOTOGRAPHSRECIEPTSB
EVERAGECOASTERSMATCHBOOKSLEAVESBROC
HURESPAPER CURRENCYSUBWAY TICKETSMUSEU
M PASSESBUSINESS CARDSTOLLBOOTH RECIEPTS
PRESSED FLOWERSCANDY WRAPPERSMAPSWINE
LABELSLUGGAGE TAGSHOTEL STATIONARYFERRY
TICKETSPHONECARDSMOVIE & THEATER TICKETS
MENUSPASSPORT PHOTOSPARKING TICKETSTRAI
N TICKETSPHOTOGRAPHSRECIEPTSBEVERAGECO
ASTERSMATCHBOOKSLEAVESBROCHURESPAPER
CURRENCYSUBWAY TICKETSMUSEUM PASSESBUS
INESS CARDSTOLLBOOTH RECIEPTSPRESSED FLO
WERSCANDY WRAPPERSMAPSWINE LABELSLUG
GAGE TAGSHOTEL STATIONARYFERRY TICKETSPH
ONECARDSMOVIE & THEATER TICKETSMENUSPAS
SPORT PHOTOSPARKING TICKETSTRAIN TICKETSP

PASTE HERE

INTERESTING SHOPS:

ACQUISITIONS & GIFTS:

THINGS TOO LARGE, FRAGILE OR EXPENSIVE TO BUY:

NOTEWORTHY SIGHTS OR EXPERIENCES:

MEMORABLE ENCOUNTERS:

TRAIN TICKETSPHOTOGRAPHSRECIEPTSBEVERAGECOASTERSMATCHBOOKSLEAVESBROCHURESPAPER CURRENCYSUBWAY TICKETSMUSEUM PASSESBUSINESS CARDSTOLLBOOTH RECIEPTSPRESSED FLOWERSCANDY WRAPPERSMAPSWINE LABELSLUGGAGE TAGSHOTEL STATIONARYFERRY TICKETSPHONECARDSMOVIE & THEATER TICKETSMENUSPASSPORT PHOTOSPARKING TICKETSTRAIN TICKETSPHOTOGRAPHSRECIEPTSBEVERAGECOASTERSMATCHBOOKSLEAVESBROCHURESPAPER CURRENCYSUBWAY TICKETSMUSEUM PASSESBUSINESS CARDSTOLLBOOTH RECIEPTSPRESSED FLOWERSCANDY WRAPPERSMAPSWINE LABELSLUGGAGE TAGSHOTEL STATIONARYFERRY TICKETSPHONECARDSMOVIE & THEATER TICKETSMENUSPASSPORT PHOTOSPARKING TICKETSTRAIN TICKETSPHOTOGRAPHSRECIEPTSBEVERAGECOASTERSMATCHBOOKSLEAVESBROCHURESPAPER CURRENCYSUBWAY TICKETSMUSEUM PASSESBUSINESS CARDSTOLLBOOTH RECIEPTSPRESSED FLOWERSCANDY WRAPPERSMAPSWINE LABELSLUGGAGE TAGSHOTEL STATIONARYFERRY TICKETSPHONECARDSMOVIE & THEATER TICKETSMENUSPASSPORT PHOTOSPARKING TICKETSTRAIN TICKETSPHOTOGRAPHSRECIEPTSBEVERAGECOASTERSMATCHBOOKSLEAVESBROCHURESPAPER CURRENCYSUBWAY TICKETSMUSEUM PASSESBUSINESS CARDSTOLLBOOTH RECIEPTSPRESSED FLOWERSCANDY WRAPPERSMAPSWINE LABELSLUGGAGE TAGSHOTEL STATIONARYFERRY TICKETSPHONECARDSMOVIE & THEATER TICKETSMENUSPASSPORT PHOTOSPARKING TICKETSTRAIN TICKETSP

PASTE HERE

DATE: _____

_____

LOCATION:
_____
_____

LODGING:
_____
_____

TRANSPORTATION:
_____
_____
_____

PLACES VISITED:
_____
_____
_____
_____
_____
_____
_____

MEALS, RESTAURANTS, SPECIAL DISHES:
_____
_____
_____
_____
_____
_____
_____
_____

TRAIN TICKETSPHOTOGRAPHSRECIEPTSBEVERAG
ECOASTERSMATCHBOOKSLEAVESBROCHURESPA
PER CURRENCYSUBWAY TICKETSMUSEUM PASSES
BUSINESS CARDSTOLLBOOTH RECIEPTSPRESSED F
LOWERSCANDY WRAPPERSMAPSWINE LABELSLU
GGAGE TAGSHOTEL STATIONARYFERRY TICKETSP
HONECARDSMOVIE & THEATER TICKETSMENUSPA
SSPORT PHOTOSPARKING TICKETSTRAIN TICKETS
PHOTOGRAPHSRECIEPTSBEVERAGECOASTERSM
ATCHBOOKSLEAVESBROCHURESPAPER CURRENC
YSUBWAY TICKETSMUSEUM PASSESBUSINESS CA
RDSTOLLBOOTH RECIEPTSPRESSED FLOWERSCAN
DY WRAPPERSMAPSWINE LABELSLUGGAGE TAGS
HOTEL STATIONARYFERRY TICKETSPHONECARDS
MOVIE & THEATER TICKETSMENUSPASSPORT PHO
TOSPARKING TICKETSTRAIN TICKETSPHOTOGRAP
HSRECIEPTSBEVERAGECOASTERSMATCHBOOKSL
EAVESBROCHURESPAPER CURRENCYSUBWAY TIC
KETSMUSEUM PASSESBUSINESS CARDSTOLLBOO
TH RECIEPTSPRESSED FLOWERSCANDY WRAPPER
SMAPSWINE LABELSLUGGAGE TAGSHOTEL STATI
ONARYFERRY TICKETSPHONECARDSMOVIE & THE
ATER TICKETSMENUSPASSPORT PHOTOSPARKING
TICKETSTRAIN TICKETSPHOTOGRAPHSRECIEPTSB
EVERAGECOASTERSMATCHBOOKSLEAVESBROC
HURESPAPER CURRENCYSUBWAY TICKETSMUSEU
M PASSESBUSINESS CARDSTOLLBOOTH RECIEPTS
PRESSED FLOWERSCANDY WRAPPERSMAPSWINE
LABELSLUGGAGE TAGSHOTEL STATIONARYFERRY
TICKETSPHONECARDSMOVIE & THEATER TICKETS
MENUSPASSPORT PHOTOSPARKING TICKETSTRAI
N TICKETSPHOTOGRAPHSRECIEPTSBEVERAGECO
ASTERSMATCHBOOKSLEAVESBROCHURESPAPER
CURRENCYSUBWAY TICKETSMUSEUM PASSESBUS
INESS CARDSTOLLBOOTH RECIEPTSPRESSED FLO
WERSCANDY WRAPPERSMAPSWINE LABELSLUG
GAGE TAGSHOTEL STATIONARYFERRY TICKETSPH
ONECARDSMOVIE & THEATER TICKETSMENUSPAS
SPORT PHOTOSPARKING TICKETSTRAIN TICKETSP

PASTE HERE

INTERESTING SHOPS:

ACQUISITIONS & GIFTS:

THINGS TOO LARGE, FRAGILE OR EXPENSIVE TO BUY:

NOTEWORTHY SIGHTS OR EXPERIENCES:

MEMORABLE ENCOUNTERS:

TRAIN TICKETSPHOTOGRAPHSRECIEPTSBEVERAG
ECOASTERSMATCHBOOKSLEAVESBROCHURESPA
PER CURRENCYSUBWAY TICKETSMUSEUM PASSES
BUSINESS CARDSTOLLBOOTH RECIEPTSPRESSED F
LOWERSCANDY WRAPPERSMAPSWINE LABELSLU
GGAGE TAGSHOTEL STATIONARYFERRY TICKETSP
HONECARDSMOVIE & THEATER TICKETSMENUSPA
SSPORT PHOTOSPARKING TICKETSTRAIN TICKETS
PHOTOGRAPHSRECIEPTSBEVERAGECOASTERSM
ATCHBOOKSLEAVESBROCHURESPAPER CURRENC
YSUBWAY TICKETSMUSEUM PASSESBUSINESS CA
RDSTOLLBOOTH RECIEPTSPRESSED FLOWERSCAN
DY WRAPPERSMAPSWINE LABELSLUGGAGE TAGS
HOTEL STATIONARYFERRY TICKETSPHONECARDS
MOVIE & THEATER TICKETSMENUSPASSPORT PHO
TOSPARKING TICKETSTRAIN TICKETSPHOTOGRAP
HSRECIEPTSBEVERAGECOASTERSMATCHBOOKSL
EAVESBROCHURESPAPER CURRENCYSUBWAY TIC
KETSMUSEUM PASSESBUSINESS CARDSTOLLBOO
TH RECIEPTSPRESSED FLOWERSCANDY WRAPPER
SMAPSWINE LABELSLUGGAGE TAGSHOTEL STATI
ONARYFERRY TICKETSPHONECARDSMOVIE & THE
ATER TICKETSMENUSPASSPORT PHOTOSPARKING
TICKETSTRAIN TICKETSPHOTOGRAPHSRECIEPTSB
EVERAGECOASTERSMATCHBOOKSLEAVESBROC
HURESPAPER CURRENCYSUBWAY TICKETSMUSEU
M PASSESBUSINESS CARDSTOLLBOOTH RECIEPTS
PRESSED FLOWERSCANDY WRAPPERSMAPSWINE
LABELSLUGGAGE TAGSHOTEL STATIONARYFERRY
TICKETSPHONECARDSMOVIE & THEATER TICKETS
MENUSPASSPORT PHOTOSPARKING TICKETSTRAI
N TICKETSPHOTOGRAPHSRECIEPTSBEVERAGECO
ASTERSMATCHBOOKSLEAVESBROCHURESPAPER
CURRENCYSUBWAY TICKETSMUSEUM PASSESBUS
INESS CARDSTOLLBOOTH RECIEPTSPRESSED FLO
WERSCANDY WRAPPERSMAPSWINE LABELSLUG
GAGE TAGSHOTEL STATIONARYFERRY TICKETSPH
ONECARDSMOVIE & THEATER TICKETSMENUSPAS
SPORT PHOTOSPARKING TICKETSTRAIN TICKETSP

PASTE HERE

DATE:

LOCATION:

LODGING:

TRANSPORTATION:

PLACES VISITED:

MEALS, RESTAURANTS, SPECIAL DISHES:

TRAIN TICKETSPHOTOGRAPHSRECIEPTSBEVERAG
ECOASTERSMATCHBOOKSLEAVESBROCHURESPA
PER CURRENCYSUBWAY TICKETSMUSEUM PASSES
BUSINESS CARDSTOLLBOOTH RECIEPTSPRESSED F
LOWERSCANDY WRAPPERSMAPSWINE LABELSLU
GGAGE TAGSHOTEL STATIONARYFERRY TICKETSP
HONECARDSMOVIE & THEATER TICKETSMENUSPA
SSPORT PHOTOSPARKING TICKETSTRAIN TICKETS
PHOTOGRAPHSRECIEPTSBEVERAGECOASTERSM
ATCHBOOKSLEAVESBROCHURESPAPER CURRENC
YSUBWAY TICKETSMUSEUM PASSESBUSINESS CA
RDSTOLLBOOTH RECIEPTSPRESSED FLOWERSCAN
DY WRAPPERSMAPSWINE LABELSLUGGAGE TAGS
HOTEL STATIONARYFERRY TICKETSPHONECARDS
MOVIE & THEATER TICKETSMENUSPASSPORT PHO
TOSPARKING TICKETSTRAIN TICKETSPHOTOGRAP
HSRECIEPTSBEVERAGECOASTERSMATCHBOOKSL
EAVESBROCHURESPAPER CURRENCYSUBWAY TIC
KETSMUSEUM PASSESBUSINESS CARDSTOLLBOO
TH RECIEPTSPRESSED FLOWERSCANDY WRAPPER
SMAPSWINE LABELSLUGGAGE TAGSHOTEL STATI
ONARYFERRY TICKETSPHONECARDSMOVIE & THE
ATER TICKETSMENUSPASSPORT PHOTOSPARKING
TICKETSTRAIN TICKETSPHOTOGRAPHSRECIEPTSB
EVERAGECOASTERSMATCHBOOKSLEAVESBROC
HURESPAPER CURRENCYSUBWAY TICKETSMUSEU
M PASSESBUSINESS CARDSTOLLBOOTH RECIEPTS
PRESSED FLOWERSCANDY WRAPPERSMAPSWINE
LABELSLUGGAGE TAGSHOTEL STATIONARYFERRY
TICKETSPHONECARDSMOVIE & THEATER TICKETS
MENUSPASSPORT PHOTOSPARKING TICKETSTRAI
N TICKETSPHOTOGRAPHSRECIEPTSBEVERAGECO
ASTERSMATCHBOOKSLEAVESBROCHURESPAPER
CURRENCYSUBWAY TICKETSMUSEUM PASSESBUS
INESS CARDSTOLLBOOTH RECIEPTSPRESSED FLO
WERSCANDY WRAPPERSMAPSWINE LABELSLUG
GAGE TAGSHOTEL STATIONARYFERRY TICKETSPH
ONECARDSMOVIE & THEATER TICKETSMENUSPAS
SPORT PHOTOSPARKING TICKETSTRAIN TICKETSP

PASTE HERE

INTERESTING SHOPS:

ACQUISITIONS & GIFTS:

THINGS TOO LARGE, FRAGILE OR EXPENSIVE TO BUY:

NOTEWORTHY SIGHTS OR EXPERIENCES:

MEMORABLE ENCOUNTERS:

TRAIN TICKETSPHOTOGRAPHSRECIEPTSBEVERAG
ECOASTERSMATCHBOOKSLEAVESBROCHURESPA
PER CURRENCYSUBWAY TICKETSMUSEUM PASSES
BUSINESS CARDSTOLLBOOTH RECIEPTSPRESSED F
LOWERSCANDY WRAPPERSMAPSWINE LABELSLU
GGAGE TAGSHOTEL STATIONARYFERRY TICKETSP
HONECARDSMOVIE & THEATER TICKETSMENUSPA
SSPORT PHOTOSPARKING TICKETSTRAIN TICKETS
PHOTOGRAPHSRECIEPTSBEVERAGECOASTERSM
ATCHBOOKSLEAVESBROCHURESPAPER CURRENC
YSUBWAY TICKETSMUSEUM PASSESBUSINESS CA
RDSTOLLBOOTH RECIEPTSPRESSED FLOWERSCAN
DY WRAPPERSMAPSWINE LABELSLUGGAGE TAGS
HOTEL STATIONARYFERRY TICKETSPHONECARDS
MOVIE & THEATER TICKETSMENUSPASSPORT PHO
TOSPARKING TICKETSTRAIN TICKETSPHOTOGRAP
HSRECIEPTSBEVERAGECOASTERSMATCHBOOKSL
EAVESBROCHURESPAPER CURRENCYSUBWAY TIC
KETSMUSEUM PASSESBUSINESS CARDSTOLLBOO
TH RECIEPTSPRESSED FLOWERSCANDY WRAPPER
SMAPSWINE LABELSLUGGAGE TAGSHOTEL STATI
ONARYFERRY TICKETSPHONECARDSMOVIE & THE
ATER TICKETSMENUSPASSPORT PHOTOSPARKING
TICKETSTRAIN TICKETSPHOTOGRAPHSRECIEPTSB
EVERAGECOASTERSMATCHBOOKSLEAVESBROC
HURESPAPER CURRENCYSUBWAY TICKETSMUSEU
M PASSESBUSINESS CARDSTOLLBOOTH RECIEPTS
PRESSED FLOWERSCANDY WRAPPERSMAPSWINE
LABELSLUGGAGE TAGSHOTEL STATIONARYFERRY
TICKETSPHONECARDSMOVIE & THEATER TICKETS
MENUSPASSPORT PHOTOSPARKING TICKETSTRAI
N TICKETSPHOTOGRAPHSRECIEPTSBEVERAGECO
ASTERSMATCHBOOKSLEAVESBROCHURESPAPER
CURRENCYSUBWAY TICKETSMUSEUM PASSESBUS
INESS CARDSTOLLBOOTH RECIEPTSPRESSED FLO
WERSCANDY WRAPPERSMAPSWINE LABELSLUG
GAGE TAGSHOTEL STATIONARYFERRY TICKETSPH
ONECARDSMOVIE & THEATER TICKETSMENUSPAS
SPORT PHOTOSPARKING TICKETSTRAIN TICKETSP

PASTE HERE

DAY 27 DAY

DATE: _____

_____

LOCATION:
_____
_____

LODGING:
_____
_____

TRANSPORTATION:
_____
_____
_____

PLACES VISITED:
_____
_____
_____
_____
_____
_____
_____
_____

MEALS, RESTAURANTS, SPECIAL DISHES:
_____
_____
_____
_____
_____
_____
_____
_____

TRAIN TICKETSPHOTOGRAPHSRECIEPTSBEVERAG
ECOASTERSMATCHBOOKSLEAVESBROCHURESPA
PER CURRENCYSUBWAY TICKETSMUSEUM PASSES
BUSINESS CARDSTOLLBOOTH RECIEPTSPRESSED F
LOWERSCANDY WRAPPERSMAPSWINE LABELSLU
GGAGE TAGSHOTEL STATIONARYFERRY TICKETSP
HONECARDSMOVIE & THEATER TICKETSMENUSPA
SSPORT PHOTOSPARKING TICKETSTRAIN TICKETS
PHOTOGRAPHSRECIEPTSBEVERAGECOASTERSM
ATCHBOOKSLEAVESBROCHURESPAPER CURRENC
YSUBWAY TICKETSMUSEUM PASSESBUSINESS CA
RDSTOLLBOOTH RECIEPTSPRESSED FLOWERSCAN
DY WRAPPERSMAPSWINE LABELSLUGGAGE TAGS
HOTEL STATIONARYFERRY TICKETSPHONECARDS
MOVIE & THEATER TICKETSMENUSPASSPORT PHO
TOSPARKING TICKETSTRAIN TICKETSPHOTOGRAP
HSRECIEPTSBEVERAGECOASTERSMATCHBOOKSL
EAVESBROCHURESPAPER CURRENCYSUBWAY TIC
KETSMUSEUM PASSESBUSINESS CARDSTOLLBOO
TH RECIEPTSPRESSED FLOWERSCANDY WRAPPER
SMAPSWINE LABELSLUGGAGE TAGSHOTEL STATI
ONARYFERRY TICKETSPHONECARDSMOVIE & THE
ATER TICKETSMENUSPASSPORT PHOTOSPARKING
TICKETSTRAIN TICKETSPHOTOGRAPHSRECIEPTSB
EVERAGECOASTERSMATCHBOOKSLEAVESBROC
HURESPAPER CURRENCYSUBWAY TICKETSMUSEU
M PASSESBUSINESS CARDSTOLLBOOTH RECIEPTS
PRESSED FLOWERSCANDY WRAPPERSMAPSWINE
LABELSLUGGAGE TAGSHOTEL STATIONARYFERRY
TICKETSPHONECARDSMOVIE & THEATER TICKETS
MENUSPASSPORT PHOTOSPARKING TICKETSTRAI
N TICKETSPHOTOGRAPHSRECIEPTSBEVERAGECO
ASTERSMATCHBOOKSLEAVESBROCHURESPAPER
CURRENCYSUBWAY TICKETSMUSEUM PASSESBUS
INESS CARDSTOLLBOOTH RECIEPTSPRESSED FLO
WERSCANDY WRAPPERSMAPSWINE LABELSLUG
GAGE TAGSHOTEL STATIONARYFERRY TICKETSPH
ONECARDSMOVIE & THEATER TICKETSMENUSPAS
SPORT PHOTOSPARKING TICKETSTRAIN TICKETSP

PASTE HERE

DAY 27

INTERESTING SHOPS:

ACQUISITIONS & GIFTS:

THINGS TOO LARGE, FRAGILE OR EXPENSIVE TO BUY:

NOTEWORTHY SIGHTS OR EXPERIENCES:

MEMORABLE ENCOUNTERS:

TRAIN TICKETS PHOTOGRAPHS RECIEPTS BEVERAGE COASTERS MATCHBOOKS LEAVES BROCHURES PAPER CURRENCY SUBWAY TICKETS MUSEUM PASSES BUSINESS CARDS TOLLBOOTH RECIEPTS PRESSED FLOWERS CANDY WRAPPERS MAPS WINE LABELS LUGGAGE TAGS HOTEL STATIONARY FERRY TICKETS PHONECARDS MOVIE & THEATER TICKETS MENUS PASSPORT PHOTOS PARKING TICKETS TRAIN TICKETS PHOTOGRAPHS RECIEPTS BEVERAGE COASTERS MATCHBOOKS LEAVES BROCHURES PAPER CURRENCY SUBWAY TICKETS MUSEUM PASSES BUSINESS CARDS TOLLBOOTH RECIEPTS PRESSED FLOWERS CANDY WRAPPERS MAPS WINE LABELS LUGGAGE TAGS HOTEL STATIONARY FERRY TICKETS PHONECARDS MOVIE & THEATER TICKETS MENUS PASSPORT PHOTOS PARKING TICKETS TRAIN TICKETS PHOTOGRAP HS RECIEPTS BEVERAGE COASTERS MATCHBOOKS LEAVES BROCHURES PAPER CURRENCY SUBWAY TICKETS MUSEUM PASSES BUSINESS CARDS TOLLBOO TH RECIEPTS PRESSED FLOWERS CANDY WRAPPER SMAPS WINE LABELS LUGGAGE TAGS HOTEL STATI ONARY FERRY TICKETS PHONECARDS MOVIE & THE ATER TICKETS MENUS PASSPORT PHOTOS PARKING TICKETS TRAIN TICKETS PHOTOGRAPHS RECIEPTS B EVERAGE COASTERS MATCHBOOKS LEAVES BROC HURES PAPER CURRENCY SUBWAY TICKETS MUSEU M PASSES BUSINESS CARDS TOLLBOOTH RECIEPTS PRESSED FLOWERS CANDY WRAPPERS MAPS WINE LABELS LUGGAGE TAGS HOTEL STATIONARY FERRY TICKETS PHONECARDS MOVIE & THEATER TICKETS MENUS PASSPORT PHOTOS PARKING TICKETS TRAI N TICKETS PHOTOGRAPHS RECIEPTS BEVERAGE CO ASTERS MATCHBOOKS LEAVES BROCHURES PAPER CURRENCY SUBWAY TICKETS MUSEUM PASSES BUS INESS CARDS TOLLBOOTH RECIEPTS PRESSED FLO WERS CANDY WRAPPERS MAPS WINE LABELS LUG GAGE TAGS HOTEL STATIONARY FERRY TICKETS PH ONECARDS MOVIE & THEATER TICKETS MENUS PAS SPORT PHOTOS PARKING TICKETS TRAIN TICKETS P

PASTE HERE

DATE:

_____

_____

LOCATION:

_____

LODGING:

_____

TRANSPORTATION:

_____

_____

PLACES VISITED:

_____

_____

_____

_____

_____

_____

_____

MEALS, RESTAURANTS, SPECIAL DISHES:

_____

_____

_____

_____

_____

_____

_____

TRAIN TICKETSPHOTOGRAPHSRECIEPTSBEVERAG
ECOASTERSMATCHBOOKSLEAVESBROCHURESPA
PER CURRENCYSUBWAY TICKETSMUSEUM PASSES
BUSINESS CARDSTOLLBOOTH RECIEPTSPRESSED F
LOWERSCANDY WRAPPERSMAPSWINE LABELSLU
GGAGE TAGSHOTEL STATIONARYFERRY TICKETSP
HONECARDSMOVIE & THEATER TICKETSMENUSPA
SSPORT PHOTOSPARKING TICKETSTRAIN TICKETS
PHOTOGRAPHSRECIEPTSBEVERAGECOASTERSM
ATCHBOOKSLEAVESBROCHURESPAPER CURRENC
YSUBWAY TICKETSMUSEUM PASSESBUSINESS CA
RDSTOLLBOOTH RECIEPTSPRESSED FLOWERSCAN
DY WRAPPERSMAPSWINE LABELSLUGGAGE TAGS
HOTEL STATIONARYFERRY TICKETSPHONECARDS
MOVIE & THEATER TICKETSMENUSPASSPORT PHO
TOSPARKING TICKETSTRAIN TICKETSPHOTOGRAP
HSRECIEPTSBEVERAGECOASTERSMATCHBOOKSL
EAVESBROCHURESPAPER CURRENCYSUBWAY TIC
KETSMUSEUM PASSESBUSINESS CARDSTOLLBOO
TH RECIEPTSPRESSED FLOWERSCANDY WRAPPER
SMAPSWINE LABELSLUGGAGE TAGSHOTEL STATI
ONARYFERRY TICKETSPHONECARDSMOVIE & THE
ATER TICKETSMENUSPASSPORT PHOTOSPARKING
TICKETSTRAIN TICKETSPHOTOGRAPHSRECIEPTSB
EVERAGECOASTERSMATCHBOOKSLEAVESBROC
HURESPAPER CURRENCYSUBWAY TICKETSMUSEU
M PASSESBUSINESS CARDSTOLLBOOTH RECIEPTS
PRESSED FLOWERSCANDY WRAPPERSMAPSWINE
LABELSLUGGAGE TAGSHOTEL STATIONARYFERRY
TICKETSPHONECARDSMOVIE & THEATER TICKETS
MENUSPASSPORT PHOTOSPARKING TICKETSTRAI
N TICKETSPHOTOGRAPHSRECIEPTSBEVERAGECO
ASTERSMATCHBOOKSLEAVESBROCHURESPAPER
CURRENCYSUBWAY TICKETSMUSEUM PASSESBUS
INESS CARDSTOLLBOOTH RECIEPTSPRESSED FLO
WERSCANDY WRAPPERSMAPSWINE LABELSLUG
GAGE TAGSHOTEL STATIONARYFERRY TICKETSPH
ONECARDSMOVIE & THEATER TICKETSMENUSPAS
SPORT PHOTOSPARKING TICKETSTRAIN TICKETSP

PASTE HERE

INTERESTING SHOPS:

ACQUISITIONS & GIFTS:

THINGS TOO LARGE, FRAGILE OR EXPENSIVE TO BUY:

NOTEWORTHY SIGHTS OR EXPERIENCES:

MEMORABLE ENCOUNTERS:

COPYRIGHT © 2000 | BLUE LANTERN STUDIO
ALL RIGHTS RESERVED | PRINTED IN SINGAPORE

ISBN 1-883211-33-6

LAUGHING ELEPHANT BOOKS
POST OFFICE BOX 4399 | SEATTLE | 98104

DESIGN | SACHEVERELL DARLING